Time for HOMEWORK

Colleen Timoshenko

6

Book 6

Hunter Education Nightingale

HUNTER EDUCATION NIGHTINGALE

Time for Homework - Book 6

Published by:
Hunter Education Nightingale
ABN: 69 055 798 626
PO Box 547
Warners Bay NSW 2282
Ph: 0417 658 777
email: sales@huntereducationnightingale.com.au
paul@huntereducationnightingale.com.au
www.huntereducationnightingale.com.au

Cover Design: Doriana Berkovic

National Library of Australia Card No.
and ISBN 978 - 1 - 922242 - 30 - 3

F E D C B A
21 20 19 18 17 16

Time for Homework
Book 6

About this Book

Time for Homework Book 6 is the seventh in a series of seven books written to help reinforce many of the concepts, skills and understanding needed for today's school curriculum.

The series is designed as a user-friendly resource to improve a student's reading skills, knowledge of grammar, accuracy in spelling and improved word knowledge through word building activities. Questions covering the New Mathematics Curriculum complete each unit.

The book contains 30 units of work and one unit can be attempted each week. Each unit addresses the subjects outlined above and covers topics in today's environment which are relevant to the new Australian Curriculum for English and Mathematics.

As the child gains a better knowledge of language; reading, interpreting and responding to the written text develops and improves. Knowledge of grammar, punctuation and spelling, as well as mathematics is acquired by completing the set activities.

While *Time for Homework* treats many of the topics presented in the school curriculum, it is a summary only of those subjects. This book is fun to use at home, with the child, as a resource, to develop and improve learning.

Message to Parents

With Time for Homework, Book 6, your child should not need help with reading or the explanation of instructions. As a parent you are asked to support your child's learning but resist the temptation to provide answers. By all means, read a word for your child if necessary and then support him/her to gain a better knowledge about the word and its meaning. This reassures the child and enables one to become a more independent learner. As the child works through the book your encouragement may be all that is needed.

Regular homework helps your child develop skills which will assist in the learning process and improve confidence over time. A confident and skilled learner will enjoy school.

Praise your child at all times because you are the ideal support person in your child's life. Use this book together to make the learning process more meaningful for both of you.

Time for Homework, Book 6 is designed as a fun book for home use. Enjoy the journey!

Narrative

My Life as a Twenty Dollar Note

I have always been a popular note. That doesn't mean I particularly like being popular. No. It simply means that people are happy when they have a few of me in their pocket. But, I would like to see myself being popular for a number of different reasons. I think my colour is particularly appealing to most people and they are only too happy to feel my texture and smell my unusual scent, acquired during printing and handling by many people in my lifetime.

Just the other day, I found myself being folded and then folded again to fit into his pocket. Now I am a really tolerant person, usually. But that treatment did not make the cut. It was so unacceptable that I was hoping I could squeeze my way out of that dark, smelly pocket. Then to add insult to injury I landed inside a whirling tub of water that evening. Really, there is no consideration given these days to those of us who make it possible for the smallest of enjoyments or modest purchases.

I can't but help wonder what injury or insult will come my way next. Maybe I will be stuck inside an ATM for an indefinite period. Maybe I will get torn or written on to see how far I travel before I return to the hands of the scribbler. Maybe I will have to endure being defaced by a shoe or skateboard because I have been unlucky to land on the footpath, blown along by the wind and left to the mercy of those around me.

Now my colour is a plus because I stand out and look bright and enticing for people to want me. I know that before that fifty and one hundred appeared I was the top dollar. Now I am further down the order I still believe my colour is appealing and anyway, if you have enough of me you can buy anything with me. I am going to stick around and give enjoyment to all my customers at ATMs or cash registers no matter where I am available.

Understanding

Use the narrative to answer each question.

a. Why do people like to have 'a few' of these notes?

____

b. What senses are used in reference to this particular currency?

____

c. What are the note's reasons for being popular?

____

d. What happened to the folded note? ______________________________

e. In what person is this narrative written? ______________________________

Interpreting

Circle **T** (true) or **F** (false) to answer correctly.

a.	The story gives the currency human like characteristic.	**T**	**F**
b.	It is good to have a lot of these notes.	**T**	**F**
c.	The colour of this note does not appeal to people.	**T**	**F**
d.	This note was once the highest ranked dollar note available.	**T**	**F**
e.	This note lost its patience with an owner.	**T**	**F**

Grammar

Common, Proper and Collective Nouns

In Australia mobs of kangaroos roam wild and flocks of sheep and herds of cattle graze the land.
Captain Cook first laid claim to our country for the British in 1770.
Captain Arthur Phillip brought the First Fleet and convict settlers with him in 1788.
Use each sentence to find

a. Common Nouns ______________________________

b. Proper Nouns ______________________________

c. Collective Nouns ______________________________

Spelling

Difficult Words to Learn:
attend compare generate imagine relax

Alphabetical Order - Write the words in AO.

____

____

Nominalisation - Write each word as a noun.

____

____

Word Building

Add the suffixes **'able'** or **'ible'** meaning **'capable of'** to each word

a. response ______________

b. service ______________

c. comfort ______________

d. manage ______________

e. convert ______________

f. predict ______________

Proof Reading

Circle each spelling error and re-write the sentence correctly on the line.

a. We bout a new chair to relx in on the verander.

____

b. They have a gud discrption of the theif.

____

Punctuation

Use a comma to separate a phrase and a colon to begin a list or before a quotation. Mark the missing commas in red and place the colons in sentences where needed.

a. We came prepared but they were ready for the party anyway.

b. They said "We will be home in time for dinner."

c. You will need three cups of sugar two tea-spoons of oil and melted chocolate.

d. There were several books available when the library opened to the public.

Rounding Off

1. Round off each number to the **nearest ten**.

a. 657 ________ **b.** 842 ________

c. 375 ________ **d.** 635 ________

e. 721 ________ **f.** 547 ________

2. Round off each number to the **nearest hundred.**

a. 657 ________ **b.** 842 ________

c. 375 ________ **d.** 635 ________

e. 721 ________ **f.** 547 ________

3. Round off each number to the **nearest thousand**.

a. 4531 ________ **b.** 6275 ________

c. 8131 ________ **d.** 6175 ________

e. 7728 ________ **f.** 4981 ________

4. Round off both factors to the nearest 100 and 10 and then write an approximate product.

a. 217 x 81 ≈ ________ **b.** 394 x 22 ≈ ________

Addition

1. Add these numbers.

a. 5 million + 8 hundred thousand + 6 thousand + 4 hundred and 10 ________

b. 4 hundred thousand + 7 thousand + 5 hundred + 6 tens + 8 ones. ________

c. 8 million + 7 thousand + 9 hundred + 5 tens + 6 ones. ________

2. Using addition strategies, find the sum of numbers in the ovals.

a.

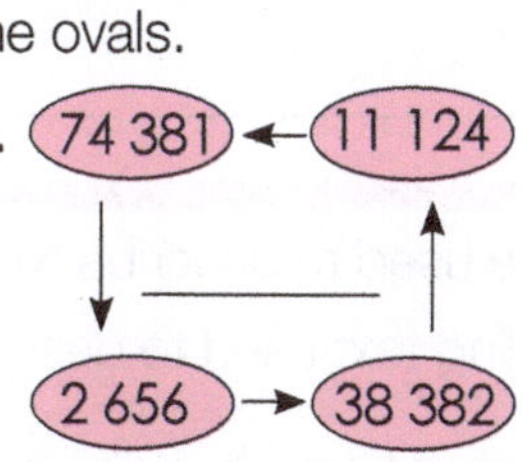

b.

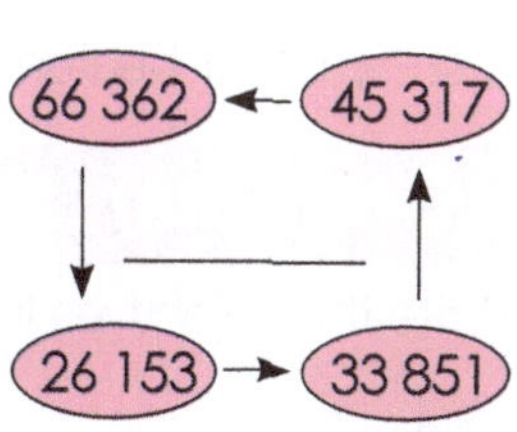

3.

a.
```
  62342
  15778
+ 12796
-------
```

b.
```
  44354
   8646
+ 32951
-------
```

c.
```
  62519
  15652
+ 22717
-------
```

Information Report

The Great Wall of China

This man-made construction was built by the Chinese as early as the 8th and 5th centuries BC. Imagine how long ago that was and yet the knowledge and skill required to build it was known even then. Sure there were no machines like we have today to assist with wall-building, but stamped earth and gravel, held between board frames, was used in its construction. These fortifications were built to keep invading hordes out of China.

Most of the ancient walls deteriorated over time and down through the centuries new walls have been constructed. Their purpose though, has not changed. Modern day construction however, has changed and while bricks and stone have replaced the rammed earth constructions the purpose for building the walls remains the same. As far back as the 14th Century, during the Ming Dynasty, some 25,000 watchtowers were built into the Wall so look-outs could warn of approaching Mongol raiders. Towards the end of the Ming, around 1600, the Wall prevented attacks to China from the Manchus.

Following China's defeat, in the First and Second Opium Wars, it opened trade with the outside world and the Wall became a great tourist attraction. The area of wall around Beijing has been frequently repaired and visitors are able to walk on that section known as The Badaling Great Wall. At this spot the Wall is approximately 7.8 metres high and 5 metres wide. But it is not an easy walk due to the steep incline from point of entry to the watchtower. The gradient is such that leg muscles are sorely tested.

While repairs have been done to areas frequented by tourists, other places are being eroded by sandstorms. So, in places, in the next decade or two, the Wall is in danger of disappearing. The most likely places where this will happen have walls built from mud rather than brick. Sections of the Wall are still being uncovered having been concealed by hills, trenches and rivers. And, as late as 2015, nine sections of the Great Wall, up to 10km in length, were discovered between two border regions of the country.

Understanding

Tick the box if the information is in the text

- a. The Great Wall was started about 6 000 years ago ☐
- b. Erosion of the Wall is caused by sandstorms. ☐
- c. Watchtowers were added 700 years ago. ☐
- d. Mongols and Manchus invaded China. ☐
- e. Early walls were made from bricks and stone. ☐
- f. Tourists are able to walk on the Wall. ☐
- g. It is not easy to walk on the Wall. ☐
- h. Within ten years some of the Wall will disappear. ☐
- i. The Ming were Chinese rulers. ☐
- j. The ancient Chinese people were very clever. ☐

Interpreting

Match a word to its meaning

WORD BANK: eroded, gradient, sorely, concealed, fortifications, deteriorated, hordes, trenches

- a. covered up ____________
- b. wasted away ____________
- c. degree of incline ____________
- d. strengthen against attack ____________
- e. greatly, very much ____________
- f. multitudes of people ____________
- g. weather-beaten ____________
- h. channels ____________

Grammar

Adjectives used to describe Nouns

Write the adjectives in the reading text used to describe each noun.

- a. ____________ constructions
- b. ____________ hordes
- c. ____________ earth
- d. ____________ walls
- e. ____________ border regions
- f. ____________ earth
- g. ____________ incline
- h. ____________ Wars
- i. ____________ raiders
- j. ____________ muscles
- k. ____________ sections

Spelling

Difficult Words to Learn:

confidence governance hesitance importance reliance

Syllabification: Write each word in syllables.

____

____

Change each difficult word from a noun to a verb.

____

____

Word Building

Make words using the suffixes **'er'** OR **'or'**

a. one who carves stone ________________

b. one who measures land ________________

c. one who teaches ________________

d. one who swims ________________

e. one who performs on stage ________________

f. one who is skilled in law ________________

Punctuation

The Apostrophe Re-write each sentence using the apostrophe in words where necessary.

a. Its going to rain tonight. ________________________________

b. Ill use the phone to call home later. ________________________________

c. Theyre not sure if itll be screened later. ________________________________

d. I know Ill be happy to finish this book. ________________________________

e. He mustnt go past the yellow lines. ________________________________

Place Value

1. Write the number showing on each abacus.

a.

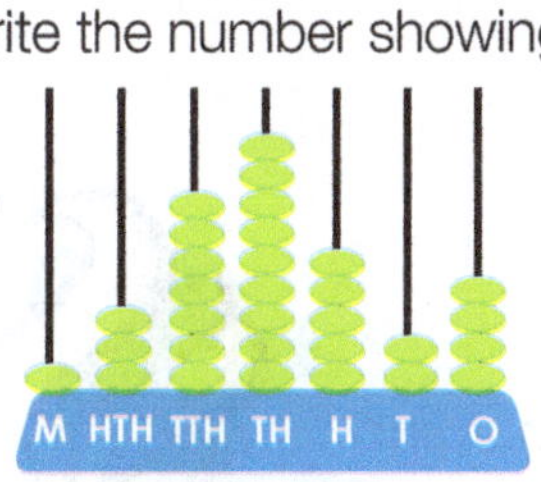

b.

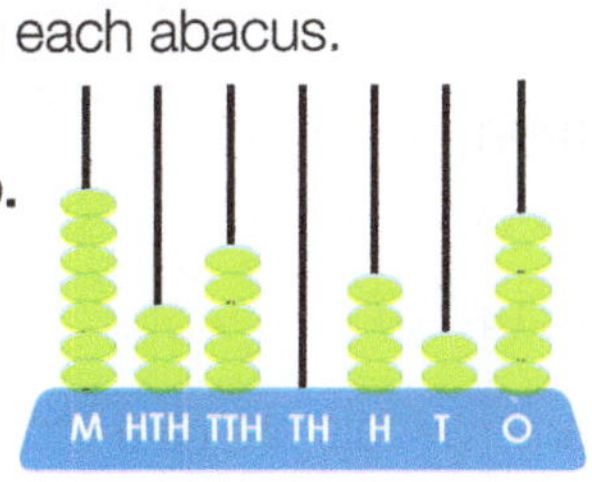

______________ ______________

2. Write millions, hundred thousands, ten thousands, thousands, hundreds, tens or ones according to place value for the circled numbers.

a. 4 6 3 (7) 2 1 8 ____________________

b. 6 7 8 3 (5) 1 9 ____________________

c. 2 (4) 0 3 0 1 7 ____________________

d. 6 8 4 1 9 3 (8) ____________________

e. (3) 3 3 4 8 2 1 ____________________

3. Write the number 150 **more** than each of these.

a. 6 253 854 ____________________

b. 7 443 667 ____________________

c. 8 135 026 ____________________

Subtraction

1. Complete each subtraction algorithm.

a. 4517 − 1302 = ______

b. 5468 − 2254 = ______

c. 3879 − 1646 = ______

2. Trade ones, tens and hundreds to find the difference in these five-digit algorithms.

a. 62535 − 10456 = ______

b. 24687 − 11599 = ______

c. 68544 − 12765 = ______

d. 39567 − 14388 = ______

3. Find the difference between each sum of money.

a. $276.58 − $113.47 = ______

b. $458.73 − $127.88 = ______

c. $389.55 − $249.84 = ______

4. A farmer had 12 265 sheep to shear. If 7 388 were already shorn, how many were left to shear?

____

The Modern-Day Olympic Games

The modern-day Olympics began back in 1894 when a committee was established to plan and organise their re-introduction. Modern-day Olympics are a revival of the Ancient Olympian Games and were first run in 1896. An International Olympic Committee (IOC) was established to organise and manage the games which were held first in Athens, Greece. Held every four years, the IOC decides where that will be. The only break in the games has been during World War 1, in 1916 and during World War 11 in 1940 and 1944.

Because the games need to be run at special venues there is a lot of preparation needed beforehand to host them. A host country might have to build stadiums, swimming pools even athletic tracks, as well as villages to accommodate all the visiting athletes. It takes time, money and labour to develop a site.

Before the games begin there is an opening ceremony and all the competing athletes from the competing Nations dress in their Olympic Uniform and parade into the stadium behind their country's flag.

The team leading the parade is the Greek team and the last team is from the host Nation. This is a chance for all athletes to come together for the raising of the Olympic flag and the lighting of the Olympic cauldron. A closing ceremony is held too and doves are released to symbolise the spirit of the games.

There are Summer Olympics and Winter Olympics and competition is open to athletes from many nations. Both men and women athletes compete in a variety of summer and winter sports and more sports are included in each year of the games. Australia prepares athletes for many of the sporting events and they bring home gold, silver and bronze medals. Each Olympic Games provides opportunities for more of our sports men and women to become National heroes and represent their country on the medal dais. After each event a ceremony is held for the first, second and third-place finishers to receive their medals. Flags of the winners' countries are raised and the national anthem of the country of the first medallist is played. Each athlete congratulates the other and joins in the excitement and happiness of the occasion.

Understanding

Shade the bubble for the best answer.

a. The Olympic Games are held every
- ◯ two years
- ◯ three years
- ◯ four years
- ◯ five years

b. The Modern-day Olympics were first held in
- ◯ 1894
- ◯ 1896
- ◯ 1900
- ◯ 1914

c. Which word is a synonym for dais?
- ◯ table
- ◯ podium
- ◯ step
- ◯ rack

d. How many medals are given for each event?
- ◯ one
- ◯ two
- ◯ three
- ◯ four

Interpreting

Write an answer to each question

a. Who is in charge of the Olympic Games? ______________________________

b. What is needed to host the Olympics? ______________________________

c. Where were the first modern-day Olympics held? ______________________________

d. What happens to symbolise the spirit of the games? ______________________________

Grammar

Abstract Nouns These nouns are ideas and feelings. Some examples are – sadness, joy, happiness

Underline the abstract nouns in each sentence. Write the noun on the line.

a. The celebration was beyond all imagination. ______________________

b. Their friendship was beneficial for the whole group. ______________________

c. Our wisdom, imagination and honesty always help us. ______________________

Spelling

Difficult Words to Learn:

judgment **obedient** **punishment**
confident **attachment**

Change each word to a verb.

____

____

____

Dictionary Work

Write the word that comes first in the dictionary.

a. maintenance, maintain ______________________

b. obey, obedient ______________________

c. questionable, question ______________________

d. punished, punishment ______________________

e. responsible, response ______________________

Word Building

Words that make sounds - **'Wh'** words.
Write a noun that might make each sound.

a. whizz ______________________

b. whimper ______________________

c. whistle ______________________

d. wail ______________________

e. whine ______________________

f. wheeze ______________________

g. whirr ______________________

h. whisper ______________________

Punctuation

The Hyphen These compound adjectives are written using a hyphen

red-hot large-scale icy-cold 75-year-old second-class third-rate heavy-handed short-winded

Use each correctly in a sentence.

a. The water was ______________________.

b. It was a ______________________ performance.

c. There was a ______________________ hunt for the killer.

d. The fire was ______________________.

e. The two men were ______________________ veterans.

f. They are ______________________ citizens.

g. The cook was ______________________ with the salt.

h. Athletes can get ______________________.

Prime Numbers

1. Circle only the prime numbers.

2 3 4 5 7 9 11 13
17 19 21 23 29 31 35

2. Write the factors for each number.

a. 8 ☐ ☐ ☐ and ☐

b. 16 ☐ ☐ ☐ ☐ and ☐

c. 24 ☐ ☐ ☐ ☐ ☐ ☐ ☐ and ☐

d. 28 ☐ ☐ ☐ ☐ ☐ and ☐

3. How many prime numbers between zero and 20? ☐

4. What is the sum of the prime numbers between zero and 20? ☐

Multiplication

1. Use the contracted method to complete each multiplication.

a. 1234 x 3 = ______

b. 1814 x 7 = ______

c. 3805 x 5 = ______

d. 24682 x 4 = ______

e. 33127 x 6 = ______

f. 16537 x 3 = ______

2. Complete the multiplication web.

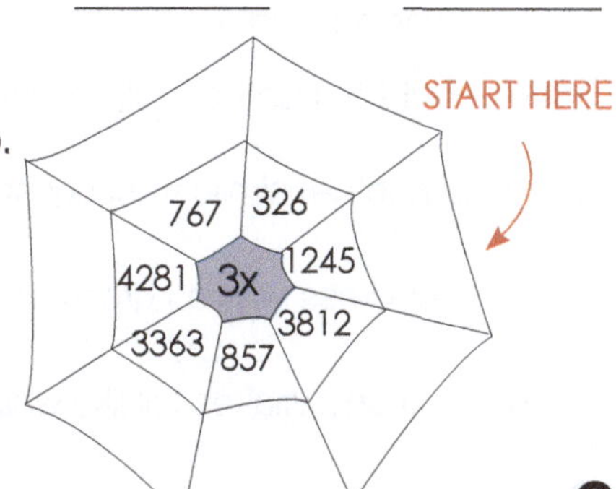

The Olympic Flag and Rings

The Olympic Rings are very symbolic. They were designed by a French Baron in 1912. He was a member of the International Olympic Committee (IOC). The flag and rings represent all nations competing in the Olympic Games. The flag is flown at all summer and winter Olympic Games and is an important part of these events just as much as the Olympic cauldron.

The Olympic Flag is white with five, interlocking, coloured rings representing the five continents from which the athletes travel to compete in the games. The rings have at least one colour from every nation's flag in them. The five colours are: blue, black, red on the top and yellow and green in between on the bottom. This flag has been used at every Olympic event since 1920.

Understanding

Tick the box if you can find this information in the text.

a. There is an acronym in the text. ☐

b. The Olympic Flag is white. ☐

c. There are five, interlocking rings on the flag. ☐

d. All nations are represented on the Olympic Flag. ☐

e. The Olympic Flag flies at all Olympic Games. ☐

f. There are two types of Olympic Games. ☐

g. The flag's designer was French. ☐

h. The flag is as important as the Olympic torch. ☐

Interpreting

Write an answer to each question

a. Who organises the Olympic Games? ______________________

b. What do the colours of the rings represent? ______________________

c. Which colour do you think best represents Australia? ______________________

d. What is the meaning of 'very symbolic' in this text? ______________________

e. What is the Olympic cauldron? ______________________

Grammar

Similes – Used to compare one thing to another using: like or as … as

Underline the similes used in each sentence.

a. The day was like burning lava.

b. They were as thick as thieves.

c. It was as cold as ice.

d. The boys were silent like stone.

e. It bubbled up like boiling water.

f. It moved silently like a snake.

Now write another simile to suggest a similar image to the ones in each sentence.

a. Her dress was as green as a cucumber. ______________________

b. Soft snowflakes fell like white powder. ______________________

c. The baby was as sweet as honey. ______________________

Spelling

Difficult Words to Learn:

significance **sufficient** **television** **wondrous** **attention**

Alphabetical Order - Write the words in AO.

____

____

Change each word from a noun to a Verb.

____

____

Proof Reading

Circle each spelling error and re-write the sentence correctly on the line.

a. Meny nations have athlets competiting in the Olympic Games.

____

b. The Olympic Rings are deesined to reprsent five coninents.

____

Word Building

Abstract Nouns

envious, knowledge, patriotism, narcissism

Match each word to its meaning.

a. Love of country ______________

b. The power of understanding ______________

c. A feeling of envy ______________

d. The feeling of self-importance ______________

Write a noun meaning:

a. a place where stone is obtained. ______________

b. people at a concert. ______________

c. people in church ______________

d. a list of books ______________

Punctuation

The Semi-Colon – Join two independent clauses about the same thing.

Place the semi-colon correctly in each sentence.

a. There could be rain tomorrow you should check then.

b. The Olympic Flag is white it has five interlocking coloured rings too.

Square Numbers

1. Write the square numbers shown by each of these groups.

a. 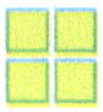

b. 

c. 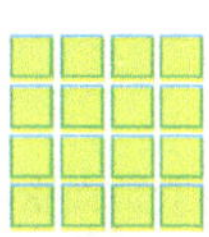

d. 

e. 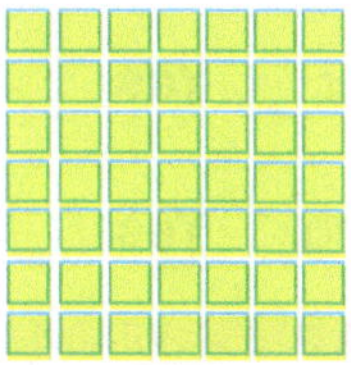

f. 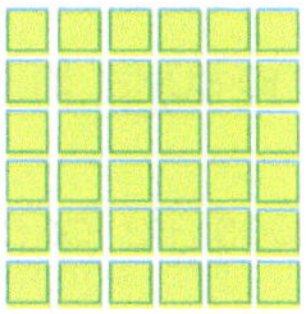

2. Complete the table of square numbers.

6^2	10^2	5^2	8^2	11^2	9^2

3. Complete each number sentence.

a. $6^2 - 7 =$ ☐ **b.** $8^2 + 7 =$ ☐ **c.** $5^2 + 2^2 =$ ☐

d. $7^2 + 4^2 =$ ☐ **e.** $3^2 + 9^2 =$ ☐ **f.** $10^2 - 9^2 =$ ☐

Division

1. Complete these divisions, with remainders.

a. 3)172 r **b.** 2)303 r **c.** 5)176 r

d. 6)385 r **e.** 4)273 r **f.** 7)527 r

2. Write the algorithm for each number sentence and then find the answer and remainder.

a. 847 ÷ 5 = ☐ **b.** 386 ÷ 5 = ☐

c. 732 ÷ 6 = ☐ **d.** 856 ÷ 4 = ☐

3. Complete each algorithm, NB. Zeros.

a. 3)4023 r **b.** 4)2305 r **c.** 6)5047 r

Procedure

Damper

Ingredients:

2 cups of self-raising flour
A generous pinch of salt
2 teaspoons sugar
1 tablespoon butter
1 cup milk

Method:

Sift the flour and salt and add sugar
Rub in the butter
Mix in the milk to make a soft dough
Knead lightly on a board until smooth
Form into a round shape and place in a tin
Glaze the top with milk
Bake in a moderate oven (1600C) for 40 minutes.
Turn out onto a tea towel, wrap and cool.

Serve warm with soup for lunch or dinner.

Bush Brownies

Ingredients:

1 ½ cups of self-raising flour
¼ cup butter
½ cup of brown sugar
2 cups of mixed fruit
1 egg
1 cup of milk

Method:

Sift dry ingredients into a bowl
Rub in the butter
Add the mixed fruit
Mix in the well beaten egg and milk.
Pour into a greased slice tin
Bake in a moderate oven (1600C) for 35 minutes.

Serve sliced and buttered.

Serve to visitors or enjoy for afternoon tea.

Understanding

Shade the bubble for the best answer.

a. All lines in the method begin with

- ◯ A noun
- ◯ An adjective
- ◯ An adverb
- ◯ A verb

b. The purpose of this text is to

- ◯ inform
- ◯ instruct
- ◯ entertain
- ◯ persuade

c. The oven needs to be

- ◯ not too hot or too cold
- ◯ not too cold or too warm
- ◯ not too hot and not warm
- ◯ not too hot just moderate

d. Which word is the best substitute for 'ingredients'?

- ◯ makings
- ◯ elements
- ◯ contents
- ◯ materials

Interpreting

Circle **Yes** or **No** to answer each point.

a. These recipes would be easy to make. **Yes** **No**

b. I would like to make these recipes. **Yes** **No**

c. A damper is made to replace bread. **Yes** **No**

d. There is an egg in each recipe. **Yes** **No**

e. Both recipes take the same time to cook. **Yes** **No**

f. There is no sugar in the Damper. **Yes** **No**

g. Both recipes need a moderate oven. **Yes** **No**

h. The recipes are for country living. **Yes** **No**

Grammar

Metaphors – One thing is said to be the other.

Match column A with column B to make metaphors. Write each one on the line.

Column A	Column B
a. The stars	**g.** the salt of the earth. ______
b. The camel	**h.** has the heart of a lion. ______
c. The athlete	**i.** are like diamonds. ______
d. The mouse	**j.** is swift of foot. ______
e. The robber	**k.** is a ship of the desert. ______
f. He is	**l.** has the cunning of a fox. ______

Spelling

Difficult Words to Learn:

conclude encourage favour acknowledge attach

Nominalisation: Write the difficult words as nouns.

____

Alphabetical Order: Write the difficult words in AO.

____

Missing Letters: Fill in the missing letters.

a. e n c ___ ___ r ___ g ___ m ___ n t

b. ___ c k n ___ w l ___ d g ___ **c.** f ___ v ___ ___ r ___ b l ___

d. c ___ n c l ___ d ___ **e.** ___ t t ___ c h

f. ___ n c ___ ___ r ___ g ___

g. Are the missing letters consonants or vowels? ______________

Word Building

The Prefix 'fore' meaning before or in front. Write words using 'fore' as a prefix.

a. ward ______________

b. go ______________

c. finger ______________

d. head ______________

e. cast ______________

f. shore ______________

g. close ______________

h. shadow ______________

i. sight ______________

Punctuation

Ellipsis Points (three dots) shows omission of text, suspense or time delay.

Identify how an ellipsis is used in the examples by writing: O. S or TD on the line.

a. Oh! No! … ______________ **b.** anyway … ______________ **c.** Who is calling?… ______________

d. They were ahead at half-time … what happened? ______________

Integers

1. Write the integers for the range shown on each number line.

a. -6 0+1

b. -2 0 +3

c. -12 -5

d. -50 0 20

2. Complete the addition and subtraction of these integers.

a. -6+7 = ☐ **b.** +5-9 = ☐

c. -7+3 = ☐ **d.** -8+3 = ☐

e. +7-12 = ☐ **f.** +8-11 = ☐

3. Colour the value of the integer on each line.

a. -7 (-5 0 +5)

b. -30 (-50 0 +50)

c. +9 (-5 0 +5)

d. -250 (-500 0 +500)

Fractions

1. Write the equivalent fraction for each of these.

a. $\frac{4}{10}$ = ☐ **b.** $\frac{6}{8}$ = ☐ **c.** $\frac{30}{50}$ = ☐

d. $\frac{4}{8}$ = ☐ **e.** $\frac{5}{10}$ = ☐ **f.** $\frac{3}{12}$ = ☐

g. $\frac{2}{6}$ = ☐ **h.** $\frac{2}{8}$ = ☐ **i.** $\frac{6}{10}$ = ☐

2. To add fractions, both denominators must be the same. Change the denominators then add each fraction.

a. $\frac{1}{2} + \frac{1}{4} =$ ☐ $+ \frac{1}{4} =$ ☐

b. $\frac{2}{5} + \frac{1}{10} =$ ☐ $+ \frac{1}{10} =$ ☐

c. $\frac{5}{8} + \frac{1}{4} =$ $\frac{5}{8} +$ ☐ $=$ ☐

d. $\frac{2}{3} + \frac{1}{6} =$ ☐ $+ \frac{1}{6} =$ ☐

e. $\frac{3}{4} + \frac{1}{8} =$ ☐ $+ \frac{1}{8} =$ ☐

f. $\frac{3}{10} + \frac{2}{5} =$ $\frac{3}{10} +$ ☐ $=$ ☐

Let's Try Cinquain

Cinquain, pronounced 'sin – cane', is easy to write.
Just five lines long with a few words in each.
the first and last line has two syllables and
four, six and eight in the middle three lines.
Remember, 24682 and there you have
the structure for a cinquain. The best cinquains
tell a small story where something happens.
Pick your topic to begin.

A cinquain makes a pattern like a diamond.
Here is one to show you how.

Knitting
Needles
making noises
knit one, purl one, slip one
that's how to make a warm jumper
Knitting

Start your poems here.

Understanding

Shade the bubble for the best answer

a. What is the origin of the word 'cinquain'

- ◯ English ◯ German
- ◯ French ◯ Spanish

b. How many syllables in the fourth line of a cinquain?

- ◯ two ◯ four
- ◯ six ◯ eight

c. What stitch is used to make a jumper?

- ◯ knit and purl ◯ purl and slip
- ◯ knit and slip ◯ knit, purl, slip

d. What shape does cinquain writing have?

- ◯ diamond ◯ square
- ◯ triangular ◯ circular

Interpreting

Circle **Yes** or **No** to answer each statement.

a. Cinquains do not have to rhyme.	**Yes**	**No**
b. Counting syllables on each line is important in cinquains.	**Yes**	**No**
c. There is a definite pattern formed when writing cinquains.	**Yes**	**No**
d. Cinquains tell a story where there is an action.	**Yes**	**No**
e. Cinquain is pronounced as 'sin cane'.	**Yes**	**No**

Grammar

Personification – To take on human characteristics.

Follow the example and write an additional response using each starting point.

a.	The moon	walks with steps of silence.	The moon ______
b.	The boat	swims with broad strokes.	The boat ______
c.	Our cat	sings with mellow voice	Our cat ______
d.	Dogs	whistle and cry at night	Dogs ______
e.	The wind	pirouettes through the sky	The wind ______

Spelling

Difficult Words to Learn:

introduce **intend** **imagine**
inform **limit**

Re-write each word using the suffix - **tion, ion,** or **ation** - (sounds like 'shun')

____

____

Alphabetical Order: Write the difficult words in AO.

____

____

Scrambled Words: Write each word correctly

a. troinduce ______ **b.** ioninnett ______

c. miitli ______ **d.** inimeag ______

e. endtin ______ **f.** mrofin ______

Word Building

Compound Words

Build a compound word from these short words.

stand, wood, keeper, stick, works, stand, under, broom, fire, goal, grand, fire

a. ______

b. ______

c. ______

d. ______

e. ______

f. ______

Punctuation

Brackets – Used to enclose information or additional comments.

Place brackets around the additional information in each sentence.

a. The International Olympic Committee IOC manages the Olympic Games.

b. Random access memory RAM is a technological term.

c. Mr Gough Whitlam 1916-2015 was the Prime Minister of Australia.

Equivalent Fractions

1. Write the equivalent fraction below each

a. 0.1 **b.** 0.7 **c.** 0.5 **d.** 0.2 **e.** 0.6

f. 0.9 **g.** 0.3 **h.** 0.25 **i.** 0.75 **j.** 0.8

2. Circle the number that is NOT an equivalent fraction.

a. $\frac{1}{2}$, 50%, 0.2 **b.** $\frac{1}{2}$, 50%, 0.4

c. $\frac{7}{10}$, 75%, $\frac{3}{4}$ **d.** $\frac{2}{5}$, 20%, 0.4

e. $\frac{1}{3}$, $\frac{3}{5}$, 60% **f.** 80%, 0.4, $\frac{4}{5}$

3. Add the missing fractions.

a.

0.3		0.7

b.

0.7		0.8

Decimals and Fractions

1. Add the missing fractions.

a.

0.2		0.4			0.7	0.8		1

b.

$\frac{1}{8}$	$\frac{1}{4}$		$\frac{1}{2}$			$\frac{7}{8}$	1

2. Match each fraction to its position on the number line.

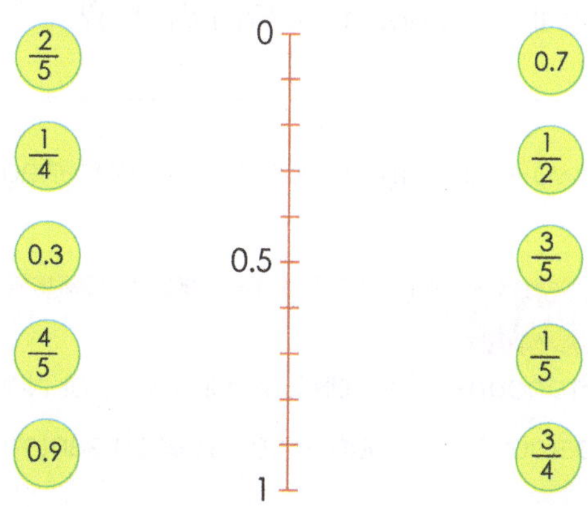

3. Write the fraction coloured on each shape.

a.  **b.** 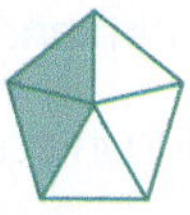 **c.** 

The Australian Flag

In 1901 a public design competition was held so the Australian people could choose the design for their new flag. That design is still in use today and the flag can be seen flying daily on all government and semi-government buildings. Other important structures, like the Sydney Harbour Bridge, also fly the flag. The flag was first raised on 3 September 1901 and this date is celebrated annually as Australian National Flag Day.

The Australian National Flag can be divided into four quadrants with a mixture of crosses and stars on a blue background each representing significant reminders of our history and place in the universe. The three crosses of St George, St Andrew and St Patrick, forming the Union Jack, are seen in the top, left quadrant and are a reminder of our past ties to the British Empire from where our laws and parliamentary democracy, as well as freedom of speech and human rights and responsibilities derive. The constellation of the Southern Cross marks our position in the southern hemisphere. This constellation also relates to Indigenous legends of our Aboriginal and Torres Strait Islander peoples. The seven pointed star represents the six states and all of the federal territories that form the Commonwealth of Australia.

Here are the flags used in the Union Jack, which is in the top, left quarter of the Australian Flag.

England

+

Scotland

+

Ireland

=

Current Union Flag (1801)

Southern Cross

Commonwealth Star

Understanding

Tick the box if the information is in the text.

a. The Union Jack is part of the Australian Flag. ☐

b. The Australian Flag was designed in 1901. ☐

c. The flag design was chosen by the people. ☐

d. There is an Australian National Flag Day. ☐

e. The Union Jack is made up of three crosses. ☐

f. Australia belongs to the British Empire. ☐

g. Australian laws are the same as British laws. ☐

h. The Commonwealth Star has seven points. ☐

i. The Southern Cross is a large constellation. ☐

j. All buildings fly the flag each day. ☐

Interpreting

Write an answer to each question.

a. What Australian values does the flag represent?

____

b. Why is the Southern Cross part of the flag?

____

c. What are the colours of the English Flag?

____

d. Which two flags in the Union Jack have a diagonal cross?

____

Grammar

Personal Pronouns – Words Used in Place of Nouns **I, me, we, us, you, he, she, it, him, her, they, them**

Circle the personal pronouns used in each sentence.

a. Bec and I will be with them all night,

b. He and she were looking after them for the day.

c. Give the books to him and her.

d. You were late but they could not wait for you.

Use the correct pronoun in each sentence.

e. You and __________ will be 12 soon.

f. The cat was white and __________ was black too.

Spelling

Difficult Words to Learn:

capable attentive fulfilled expensive visible

Antonyms: Re-write each word using the prefix 'un' or 'in' to form opposites.

____

____

Dictionary Work: Write the word that comes first

a. avalanche, available ____________

b. genuine, genius ____________

c. capacity, capable ____________

d. experience, expertise ____________

e. visibility, visible ____________

f. fulfilled, fulfilling ____________

Word Building

Prefix **'sub'** – meaning under

Write new words using 'sub' as a **prefix** with:

marine, mariner, scribe, side, title, way

a. ____________ **b.** ____________

c. ____________ **d.** ____________

e. ____________ **f.** ____________

Proof Reading

Circle the spelling errors in each sentence. Write the words correctly on the line.

a. They are very capible of making it an enjoyable occassion. ____________

b. We have fulfiled our dream and bout an expensve boat. ____________

Punctuation

Inverted Commas Use the correct punctuation in each sentence.

a. Ben said come here now ____________

b. why are you late asked dad ____________

c. run quickly the boy yelled ____________

Money

1. Write each fraction or decimal as a percentage.

a. $\frac{72}{100}$ = ___ % b. $\frac{18}{100}$ = ___ % c. $\frac{48}{100}$ = ___ %

d. $\frac{1}{2}$ = ___ % e. $\frac{3}{4}$ = ___ % f. $\frac{2}{5}$ = ___ %

g. 0.7 = ___ % h. 0.6 = ___ % i. 0.25 = ___ %

2. Write the discount price for each item.

a.

New Price $ ________

b.

New Price $ ________

c.

New Price $ ________

d.

New Price $ ________

Number Pattens

This graph can be used to show multiples of numbers.

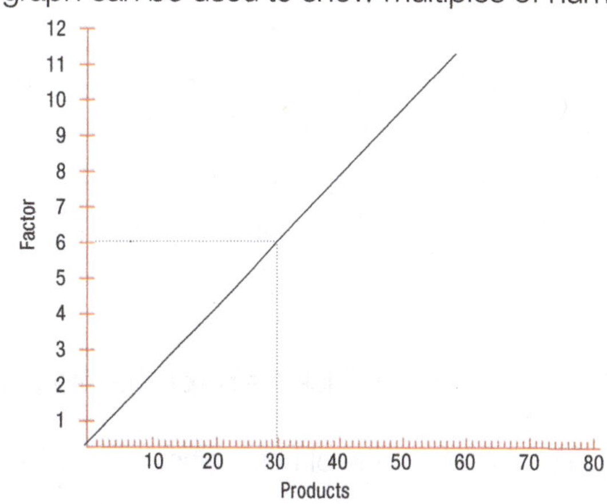

1. Show these multiples on the graph.
5 x 6 = 30 is already done.

a. 4 x 6 = ☐ **b.** 6 x 6 = ☐

c. 8 x 6 = ☐ **d.** 3 x 6 = ☐

e. 7 x 6 = ☐ **f.** 10 x 6 = ☐

2. Extend each pattern.

Rule	Pattern
+52	18, 70, ___, ___, ___
x3	3, 9, 27, ___, ___, ___
÷2	64, 32, ___, ___, ___

Taking Stock

All was quiet when the bush began to awaken that bright morning in early summer. Not long before, the shimmering glow of the sun was visible in the early morning sky and with the dawn came the added fear of what could lie ahead. From the look of things we were in for a brute of a day. There had been no rain in our catchment for weeks and the land and the dams were bone dry.

"Only need a slight piece of broken bottle to attract the sun and we'll be in for it", said Omar.

That's the trouble in this neck of the woods, it doesn't take much at all to start a fire in such dry conditions. And there's no hint of rain either – just as there hasn't been for the past month, so we all know what to expect. Life in Australia can be wonderful but when the land turns parched and is calling out for help it doesn't need a bush fire to create fear and panic in residents' hearts. Nor does it need some foolish fiend to go around lighting fires in parched bushland, where it can get away quickly into dry grasslands and burn for days on end.

"Let's get ready just in case we need to stay and fight or evacuate. In any case, we might need to put our survival plan into action today", dad suggested.

He knew what to expect on days like this and with all of his experience we knew it would be wise to listen and take heed of what he was saying. After all our lives depend on keeping a cool head and being prepared for anything that mother-nature might throw at us.

Understanding

Shade the bubble for the best answer.

a. This part of the narrative is the

- ◯ complication
- ◯ orientation
- ◯ climax
- ◯ resolution

b. What is meant by 'a brute of a day'?

- ◯ a hard fought day
- ◯ it will be a bully of a day
- ◯ there will be a lot on today
- ◯ the day will be harsh and hot

c. What does Omar suggest might happen?

- ◯ a fire might break a bottle
- ◯ heated glass could ignite the grass
- ◯ 'We'll be in for it" if the glass breaks
- ◯ there will be no problems today

d. What reasons are given that a fire might happen?

- ◯ there has been a lot of rain recently
- ◯ the land is wet and the dams are full
- ◯ people go around lighting fires in the bush
- ◯ the bushland is parched and grasslands dry

Interpreting

Tick the box if the information is in the text.

a. Omar's outlook is one of pessimism. ☐

b. Dad likes to be ready for all events. ☐

c. It is important to stay calm in a bush fire. ☐

d. Our mother might throw a lot at us. ☐

e. There are several idioms in this text. ☐

f. Dad is someone who knows what to do in a fire. ☐

g. The setting of this story is in the winter. ☐

h. The dawn sky was a glowing and shimmering red. ☐

i. In case of fire, you need a survival plan. ☐

j. Either you stay and fight a fire or evacuate. ☐

Grammar

Idioms – Expressions that can't be taken literally.

There are several idioms in 'Taking Stock' – find and match each one to its meaning.

a. being harsh and hot ______________________

b. this place or area of land ______________________

c. staying calm when things go wrong ______________________

d. natural events that come our way ______________________

Spelling

Difficult Words to Learn:

wonder industry continue danger fame

Change each difficult word to an adjective by adding the suffix **'ous'** to it.

____

____

Alphabetical Order: Write the difficult words in AO

____

____

Missing Letters: Fill in the missing letters.

a. f __ m __ __ s **b.** c __ n t __ n __ __

c. d __ n g __ r __ __ __ s

d. __ n d __ s t r __ __ __ s **e.** w __ n d r __ __ s

Word Building

A **hyphen** is used when **'all'** and **'non'** are prefixes. Join each word correctly.

electric, event, important, returnable, smoking, rounder

a. ____________________

b. ____________________

c. ____________________

d. ____________________

e. ____________________

f. ____________________

Punctuation

Broken Quotations Example: "It won't be far away," called Ryan. "I thought I saw it yesterday."

Punctuate these broken quotations.

a. be careful not to slip warned mum if you do you could break your leg

____

b. watch out for trains cried the guard I don't want another accident

____

Angles

1. Name each angle.

a. 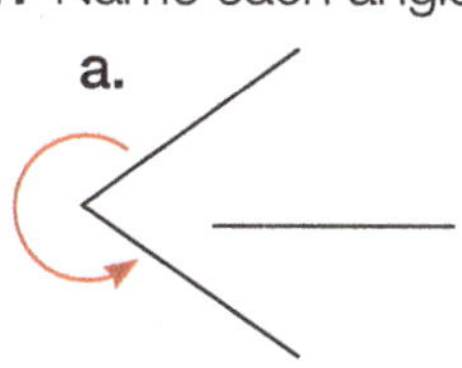 ________

b. 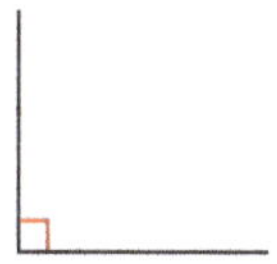 ________

c. 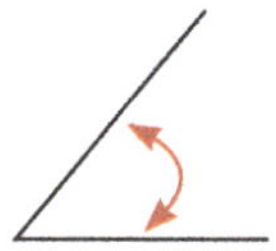 ________

d. 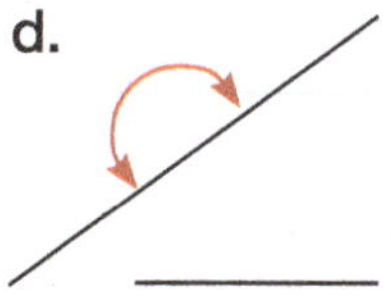 ________

e. 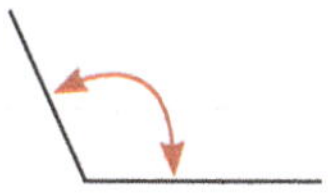 ________

f.  ________

2. Which angle is showing on each protractor?

a.  ________

b.  ________

3. The three angles of a triangle add to 180°. Find the size of the third angle.

a. 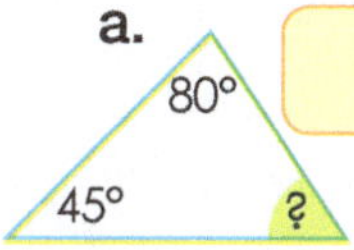

b. 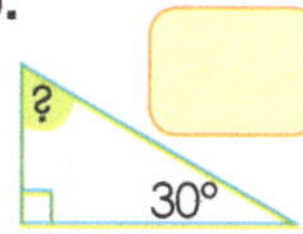

c. 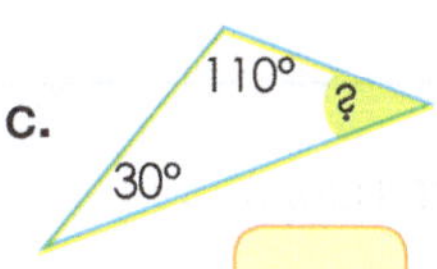

Mass

1. Use the Mass Bank to write an approximate mass for each object.

a. 

b. 

c. 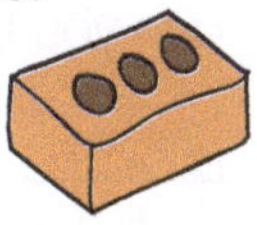

d. 

e. 

f. 

g. 

h. 

i. 

Mass Bank
2kg
500g
150T
5g
58k
3kg
1 1/2 T
20T
2g

A Twilight Bazaar

SMITHTON SCHOOL GROUNDS

WEATHER PERMITTING

FRIDAY, 15 MAY

From 4:00 pm to 9:00 pm

Lots of Fun: Best decorated bicycle or scooter · Face Painting by Dolores · Competition – Judging at 5:00 pm · For Girls and Boys- All ages

Dress up as your favourite character
Family fun-time. Judging at 6:00 pm
Best boy, best girl, best family group

Lantern and Balloon Parade at 7:00 pm
Prizes: Best decorated lantern and best design

What to Bring: A chair or rug to enjoy a family picnic or just to chill out with friends.

LOTS AND LOTS OF STALLS TO SELECT FROM: craft, clothes, jewellery, books, candles, bric-a-brac, plants, great food and much more.

Stall sites available – Contact Dori 0421 321 456 or Diane 0421123 654 to book a site.
Just $10.00 *(In case of inclement weather this Bazaar will be held in the Multi-Purpose Hall)*

Come and support your school.

Understanding

Circle **Yes** or **No** for your answer.

a. A bazzar is the same as a fete or a fair. **Yes** **No**
b. This Bazaar is to support the school. **Yes** **No**
c. There will be lots of competitions. **Yes** **No**
d. Face painting is for boys and girls. **Yes** **No**
e. Lantern design will be important. **Yes** **No**
f. There will be judging each hour. **Yes** **No**
g. Almost anything will be on sale. **Yes** **No**
h. The cost of each stall will be $20. **Yes** **No**
i. Bicycle judging is at 6:00 pm **Yes** **No**
j. This bazaar will be on Tuesday. **Yes** **No**

Interpreting

Write an answer to each question.

a. What is the meaning of 'inclement weather'?

____

b. How can you book a site to sell items at this Bazaar?

____

c. In which competition can the family win a prize? ______________________________

d. For how long will the Bazaar be running? ______________________________

e. Where is the intended venue for this Bazaar? ______________________________

Grammar

Complex Sentences – Dependent Clauses Write each simple sentence as a complex sentence.

a. The school bazaar will be on Friday. It will depend on the weather.

____

b. There will be lots of competitions. Competitions will involve different selections.

____

c. All the family can enjoy a picnic. A rug or chair will be useful.

____

Spelling

Difficult Words to Learn:

tolerant abundant significant vigilant observant

Nominalisation: Write the difficult words as nouns.
(Hint: add 'ance" to each word)

____

____

Alphabetical Order: Write the difficult words in AO

____

____

Dictionary Work: Write the word that comes **last** in the dictionary.

a. abundant, abundance ____________

b. extravagant, extravagance ____________

c. significant, significance ____________

d. arrogant, arrogance ____________

Word Building

Root Words – Duo - From the Latin meaning - **two**

Base Words: duet duo duplex dual

Show the meaning of each word.

a. two ____________

b. two-lane highway

____

c. two houses joined as one

____

d. two people performing together

____

Punctuation

Commas and Dependent Clauses Re-write each sentence using commas to separate clauses.

a. Depending on the weather there will be a Bazaar this Friday in the school grounds.

____

b. The boys and girls hung up their clothes in the cupboard before they went to bed.

____

Length

1. Write the approximate unit of length (mm, cm, m or ha) for each object.

a.  12 ______

b.  15 ______

c.  38 ______

d. 

15 ______

e.  25 ______

f. 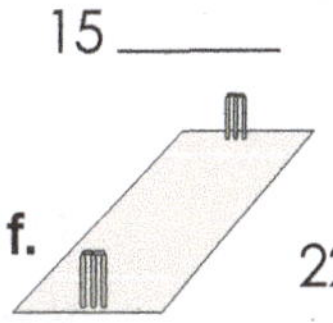 22 ______

2. Arrange each group of lengths in order, **shortest** to **longest**.

a. 47mm, 4cm, 43m, 46mm, 4km, 42m

____

b. 0.72km, 7.87m, 730cm, 989mm, 780m, 0.7km

____

3. Find the length of each line. Line scale used, 1cm = 8km.

a. ______________________________ [ ] km

b. ____________________________ [ ] km

Distance and Time

1. Use the before and after readings on each odometer to calculate the distance travelled.

a.

BEFORE

| 0 | 5 | 3 | 6 | 8 | 2 |

AFTER

| 0 | 5 | 3 | 8 | 7 | 5 |

TRIP

[ ] [ ] [ ]

b.

BEFORE

| 0 | 7 | 6 | 9 | 1 | 4 |

AFTER

| 0 | 7 | 7 | 2 | 7 | 7 |

TRIP

[ ] [ ] [ ]

2. Write the speed showing on each odometer.

a. 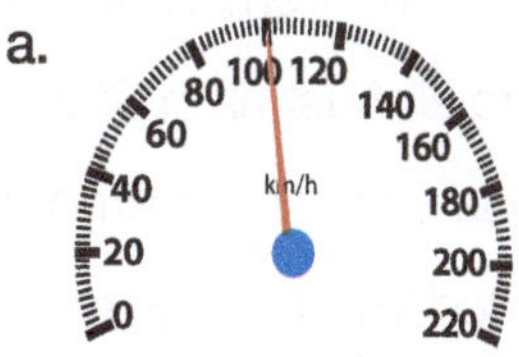

[ ]

b. 

[ ]

3. Mark the speed a car needs to travel to cover the allotted time.

a. 100 km in 1 hour

b. 120 km in 2 hours

Reading **Unit 10**

Timeline

Early Years of Australian History

1790	Second fleet of convicts arrives in Sydney Cove.
1791	Third fleet of convicts arrives.
1793	The first free settlers arrive in Sydney town.
1808	The Rum Rebellion against Governor Bligh
1824	Penal settlement founded at Redcliffe (Queensland)
1825	Establishment of Van Diemen's Land; later changed to Tasmania in 1856.
1827	Western Australia's first British settlement was made at Albany.
1829	Captain James Stirling established the first Swan River Colony.
1836 – 1842	South Australia was established as a crown colony. It was never a convict colony.
1834	The Henty Brothers landed in Portland Bay. (Victoria)
1837	John Batman settled on the site of Melbourne.
1851	Victoria separated from New South Wales
1859	Queensland separated from New South Wales. Brisbane named the capital.
1869	Darwin was established as the capital of the Northern Territory
1911	Northern Territory separates from South Australia.
1911	Australian Capital Territory established on land transferred from New South Wales
1913	Canberra named the Australian Capital City.

Understanding

Shade the bubble for the correct answer.

a. The purpose of this timeline is to
- ○ name Australian capital cities
- ○ show when states were settled
- ○ name early, major, historical events
- ○ show early penal colony dates in Australia

b. Which Australian State was first settled?
- ○ Queensland
- ○ Tasmania
- ○ New South Wales
- ○ Victoria

c. Which of these applies to South Australia?
- ○ It was the site of the first penal colony.
- ○ It was the site of a British penal colony.
- ○ It was the site of a crown colony.
- ○ It was the site of the Rum Rebellion.

d. What is the capital of Australia?
- ○ Brisbane
- ○ Darwin
- ○ Melbourne
- ○ Canberra

Interpreting

Circle **Yes** or **No** to answer each statement.

a. Early colonisation happened from 1788 – 1900.	**Yes**	**No**
b. Convicts were taken to all Australian States.	**Yes**	**No**
c. The Rum Rebellion was against Governor Bligh	**Yes**	**No**
d. Tasmania was first called Van Diemen's Land	**Yes**	**No**
e. There are 6 decades missing on the timeline.	**Yes**	**No**

Grammar

Relative Pronouns – who, whom, whose, which or that

Cross out the incorrect pronoun in each sentence.

a. (Whose / Who's) going swimming this afternoon?

b. To (who/ whom) did you give the book?

c. The train, (which / who) was late arrived at 6 pm.

d. (Whose / who's) book is on the desk?

e. The girl (that / which) came first was smart.

f. Do you know (who / whose) owns that dog?

g. Are you sure (who's / that) device is yours?

h. (Whom / who) do you know there?

Spelling

Difficult Words to Learn:

offer **develop** **frighten** **interrupt** **entertain**

Change: Verb Form – from finite to non-finite verbs by adding 'ing'

____

____

Alphabetical Order: Write the difficult words in AO.

____

____

Homophones: Words with the same sound but a different spelling and meaning. **Crews or Cruise**

Match a homophone to its meaning.

a. a sea voyage ____________

b. shipboard workers ____________

Word Building

Compound Words – Add 'where' as a suffix

Add 'where' as a suffix and write the new word on the line.

a. some ____________

b. every ____________

c. no ____________

d. any ____________

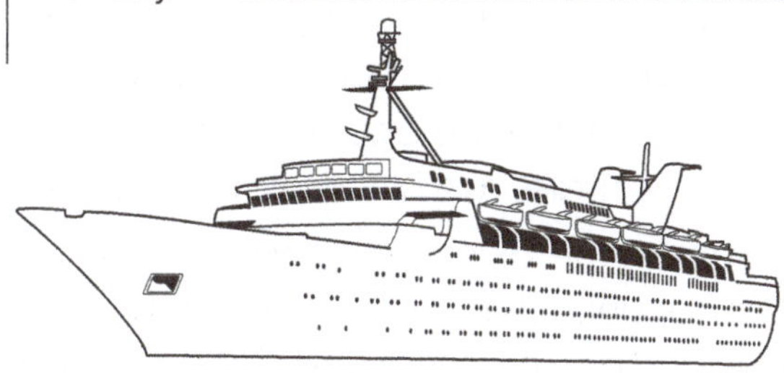

Punctuation

Quotation Marks – For titles of poems, stories and songs.

Re-write this sentence using quotation marks correctly.

a. The Man from Snowy River is a well-known Australian poem.

____

Location

Here is a map of Littleton. Use the landmarks and co-ordinates to find locations.

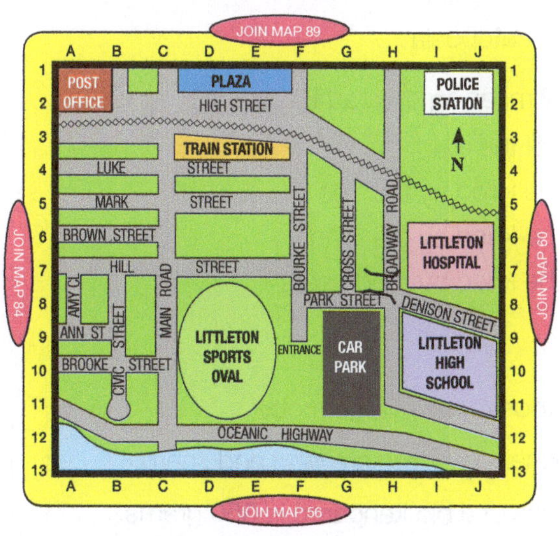

1. Give the co-ordinates for the following:

a. Post Office _____ **b.** Police Station _____

c. Plaza _____ **d.** Train Station _____

e. Hospital _____ **f.** Car Park _____

2. Name the specific landmarks at these co-ordinates.

a. D9 ____________ **b.** I10 ____________

3. In what direction does the railway line run through the town? ____________

Location

1. Make a picture graph to show this data.

Sold Cartons of Apple Juice.

Mon	Tues	Wed	Thurs	Fri	Sat	Sun
105	95	120	125	100	110	115

Picture Graph	■= cartons
Mon	
Tues	
Wed	
Thurs	
Fri	
Sat	
Sun	

2. What does a picture graph tell us?

____

3. Name three other types of graphs you could use to show this data.

____

____

The Kangaroo

Information Report

The kangaroo appears on the Australian Coat of Arms and on some Australian coins too. It is an Australian native marsupial with the red kangaroo being the largest marsupial of them all. It measures anything from 1 – 1.6 metres from its head to its rump and its tail can be another 90 to 110 centimetres in length. Its mass is around 90 kilograms. The smallest is the musky-rat kangaroo at only 15 – 20 cms long with a mass of just 340 grams.

The red kangaroo moves on its powerful hind legs which can move together or separately but they cannot move backwards. It can leap as high as 3 metres and move as far as 8 metres in one bound. It has excellent eyesight and hearing and can swivel its ears in all directions. Also, its powerful hind legs and long, sharp toenails are dangerous weapons. Just remember, old man 'roo can kill its prey in one fell swoop.

A kangaroo is a mammal as well as a marsupial which means it suckles its young in its pouch. When the young is born it looks just like a pink worm and it works its way up into the pouch and attaches itself to a milk gland where it thrives until it is big enough to leave the pouch and forage for itself. The baby is called a joey and it stays in the pouch for anything up to eighteen months depending on the climate and local conditions. A male 'roo is called a buck, boomer or old man while the female is jili.

Kangaroos are herbivores, eating grass and leaves and can survive on very little else. It is not unknown for a kangaroo to go without drinking for months at a time. They spend most of their day resting and forage for food in the night. You would be most likely to see a kangaroo on the side of the road around daylight or dusk. This is when they are out looking for food and often become road kill. Kangaroos live in groups called 'mobs' and there can be up to 100 in a mob at any one time.

Understanding

Shade the bubble that best answers each question.

a. Which statement is true?

- ◯ 'roos are small mammals
- ◯ 'roos are large marsuipals
- ◯ 'roos are large mammals
- ◯ 'roos are mammals and marsuipals

b. The expression 'old man 'roo' is an example of

- ◯ metaphor
- ◯ alliteration
- ◯ personification
- ◯ onomatopoeia

c. What action is the 'roo unable to perform?

- ◯ It can't forage for its food
- ◯ It can't suckle its young
- ◯ It can't walk backwards
- ◯ It can't swivel its ears

d. The literal meaning of 'road kill' is

- ◯ to kill the road
- ◯ to be killed by the 'roo
- ◯ to be killed by the road
- ◯ to be killed by road users

Interpreting

Tick the box if the information is in the text.

- **a.** A young kangaroo is called a joey. ☐
- **b.** Kangaroos roam in large mobs. ☐
- **c.** The red kangaroo is the largest marsupial. ☐
- **d.** The toenails of a 'roo are long and sharp. ☐
- **e.** A dollar coin has an image of a kangaroo. ☐
- **f.** The mass of a big kangaroo is 350 grams. ☐
- **g.** The musky-rat is the smallest kangaroo. ☐
- **h.** Kangaroos can go without drinking for months. ☐
- **i.** Kangaroos don't eat grass or leaves. ☐
- **j.** Kangaroos are carnivores. ☐

Grammar

Adjectives, Nouns and Noun Groups Write the nouns and noun groups in each sentence.

a. Kangaroos move on powerful hind legs. ____________________

b. The male 'roo is called a buck, boomer or old man. ____________________

c. The smallest of kangaroos is the musky-rat. ____________________

d. The kangaroo is on the Australian Coat of Arms. ____________________

e. Kangaroos live in groups called 'mobs'. ____________________

Spelling

Difficult Words to Learn:

produce measure increase gesture decide

Rule: Drop the 'e' and add 'ing' to the difficult words.

____

____

Missing Letters: Fill in the missing letters.

a. __ x p __ r __ __ n c __ **b.** p r __ d __ c __

c. m __ __ s __ r __ **d.** __ b s __ r v __

e. __ n c r __ __ s __ **f.** g __ s t __ r __

Homonyms: Words with same sound, same spelling but different meaning.

suit **suit** *pronounced (sue-t)*

a. The man had a cotton ______________ made for himself when he was in Hong Kong.

b. The law ______________ was filed today. **c.** The card player had a ______________ of diamonds.

Word Building

Compound Words – Add **'some'** as a suffix.

a. burden ______________

b. weary ______________

c. quarrel ______________

d. trouble ______________

e. worry ______________

f. whole ______________

Punctuation

Capital Letters for Holidays and Historic Events

Write each one using the correct punctuation.

a. easter ______________ **b.** christmas ______________ **c.** ramadan ______________

d. australia day ______________ **e.** new years eve ______________

Triangles

1. Draw a line from each triangle to its name.

a. 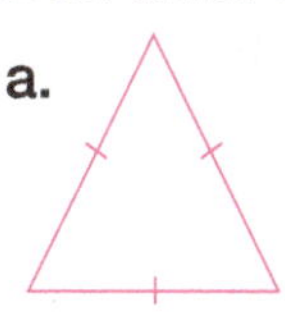

b. 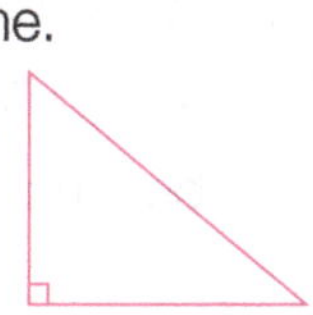

c. 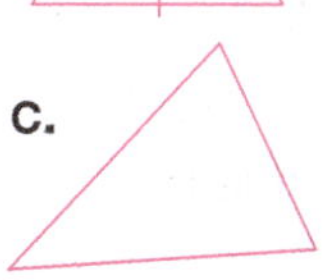

d. 

scalene

equilateral

right angle

isosceles

2. Measure the sides of each triangle. Write the perimeter and the name of each triangle.

a. 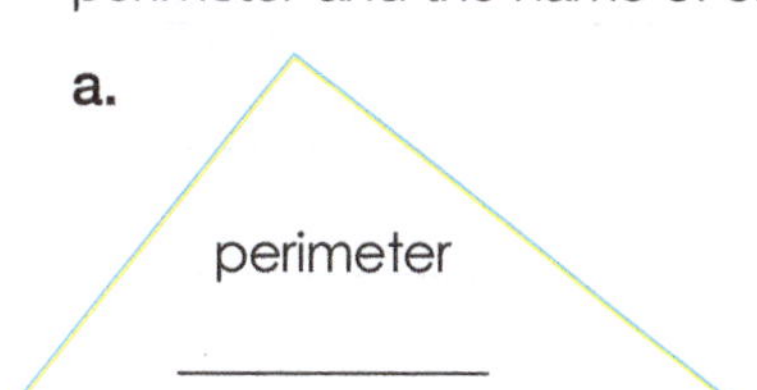

____

b. 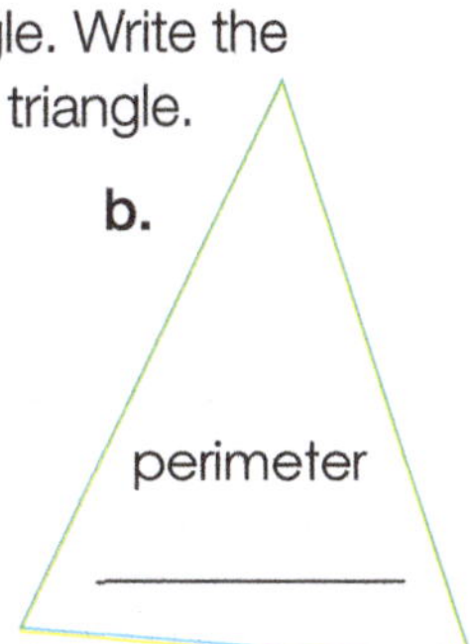

____

c. 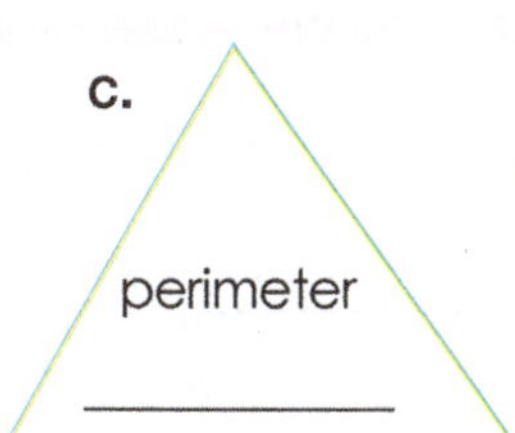

____

d. 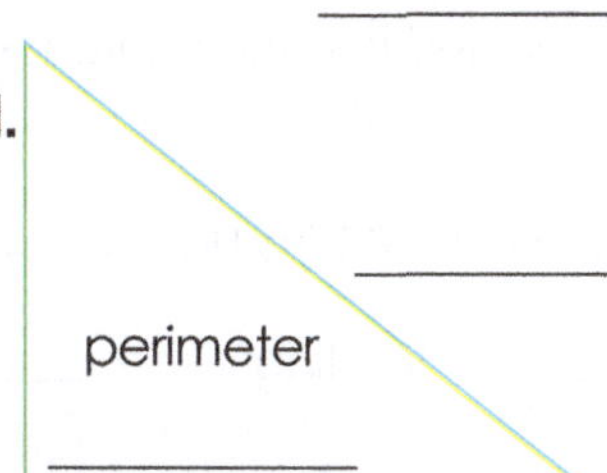

____

Circles

1. Match the distances on each circle to its name.

a. 

b. 

c. 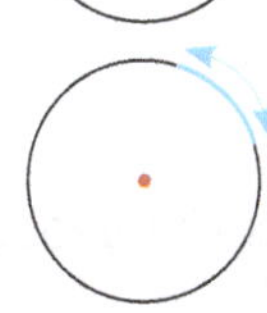

d. 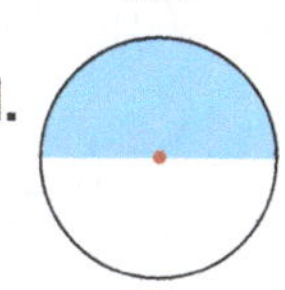

e. 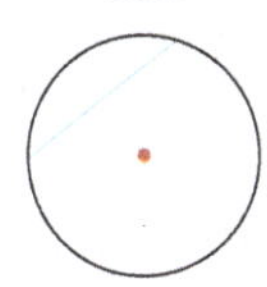

f. 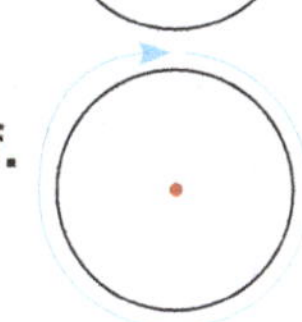

g. 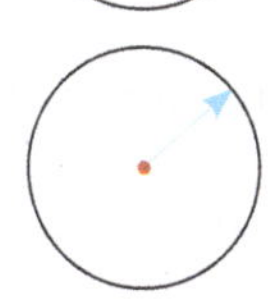

h. 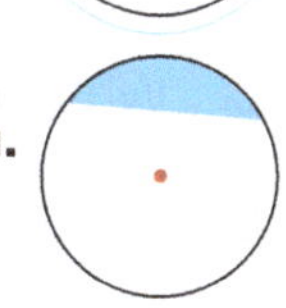

radius

diameter

circumference

quadrant

semicircle

sector

arc

chord

2. Find the size of the diameter or radius.

a. 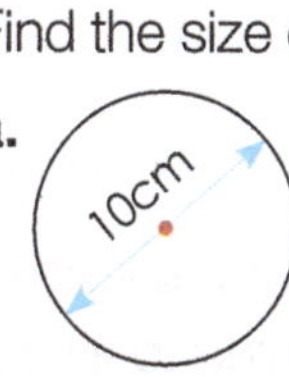

radius = ________

b. 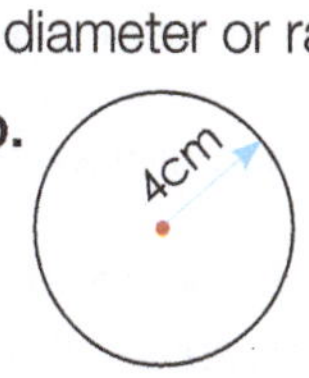

diameter = ________

c. 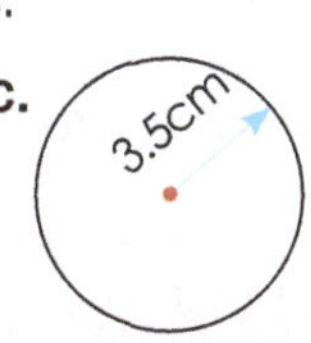

diameter = ________

3. a. Half a circle is a ______________.

b. A small section of a circle is an ______________.

The Importance of Learning to Swim

Knowing how to swim is one of the most important skills anyone can have in Australia. Why, you ask? Because we are great lovers of the beach or water sports and knowing how to swim can and does save lives. Every summer Australian beaches are packed with happy, frolicking children who need to know how dangerous the surf can be and who should be able to swim well if they are going into the water.

Many children are fortunate to have 'learn to swim' classes at school so they can be ready to enjoy a wonderful time with family and friends at the pool or the beach. However, there are some who are not so lucky and they do not know how to swim or stay out of harm's way in the water. It should be compulsory for all young children to learn how to swim. The skills they gain when they learn to swim can help them if they get into trouble in the water. Not everyone will be an Olympic swimming champion but most people can learn enough to keep themselves safe around, or in, the water.

The most important thing to remember is not to panic if something happens while swimming. And never swim alone, particularly in the river. It is also dangerous to jump into water where the depth is not known because you could hit your head on the bottom of the pool or river bed. There could also be hidden debris under the water. Things like tree branches and submerged objects are snares that can cause people to get caught or knocked out. These hidden dangers are always lurking in unknown waters. And never swim in dams because the sides are slippery and give way easily so you can be dragged under quickly and then you might not be able to get out.

So the next opportunity you have to learn to swim or improve your swimming skills take it. It could save your life or the life of someone you love. Keep an eye out for dangerous surf signs and only swim at the beach where and when it is safe to do so. Do not swim alone or jump and dive into rivers and dams. Remember, there are hidden dangers lurking in those places and you could find yourself in lots of danger.

Understanding

Shade the bubble for the best answer.

a. This purpose of this reading is to
- ◯ instruct
- ◯ inform
- ◯ persuade
- ◯ entertain

b. When is the best time to learn to swim?
- ◯ as a child
- ◯ as an adult
- ◯ before school
- ◯ after school

c. Why should you swim with someone?
- ◯ to feel safe
- ◯ to help them
- ◯ to frolic
- ◯ to get help if needed

d. Where is the most dangerous place to swim?
- ◯ in the surf
- ◯ in swimming pools
- ◯ in dams and rivers
- ◯ in waterholes

Interpreting

Write an answer to each question

a. Why should Australians learn to swim? ____________________

b. What dangers might lurk in rivers for swimmers? ____________________

c. At the beach, where should one swim? ____________________

d. When should you not swim at the beach? ____________________

e. What are the dangers of swimming in dams? ____________________

Grammar

Adverbs – Add meaning to a verb. The verb is underlined in each sentence.

Write the adverb on the line and if it tells how, when, where or why

a. We arrived late for the show. late (when)

b. They were outside playing. ____________

c. Sit there for lunch please. ____________

d. Swim between the flags. ____________

e. Run quickly to the shop. ____________

f. The bell rang after recess. ____________

Spelling

Difficult Words to Learn:

colloquial connotation community facilities immediate

Syllabification: Write each difficult word in syllables.
Hint: There are four syllables in each word.

____

____

Dictionary Work: Finish the Word to Match its Meaning.

a. col____________ informal speech

b. con____________ having another meaning

c. com____________ like-minded people

d. fac____________ buildings with a purpose

e. im____________ here and now

Word Building

Prefix **'inter'** means between

interview	interject	intercede
interfere	intersperse	intersect

Match each word to its meaning.

a. to act as go between ____________

b. where two lines cross ____________

c. to interrupt ____________

d. discussion between two people ____________

e. to meddle ____________

f. to scatter with other things ____________

Homophones: Words that sound the same but have a different spelling and meaning.

Sweet Suite Use the homophones correctly.

a. The ____________ shop is closed today. b. The lounge ____________ was bought in town.

Punctuation

Dot Points – For Items in a **List** or **Key** Points.

Eg., We need to buy:

- Scissors
- String
- Paper
- Glue

Remember the following:

- swim between the flags
- do not swim in dams
- never swim alone
- always swim with someone

Write your own key points

Number Patterns

1. Use a calculator to help you continue each number pattern.

	Rule	Pattern				
a.	x0.1	8385	838.5			
b.	x4	2	8			
c.	+150	265	415			
d.	-36	720	684			
e.	÷0.1	2	20			

2. Colour the multiples of 6 on this hundreds chart.

1	2	3	4	5	6	7	8	9	10
11	12	13	14	15	16	17	18	19	20
21	22	23	24	25	26	27	28	29	30
31	32	33	34	35	36	37	38	39	40
41	42	43	44	45	46	47	48	49	50
51	52	53	54	55	56	57	58	59	60
61	62	63	64	65	66	67	68	69	70
71	72	73	74	75	76	77	78	79	80
81	82	83	84	85	86	87	88	89	90
91	92	93	94	95	96	97	98	99	100

Fractions

1. Colour the given fraction in each shape.

a. 

$\frac{1}{2}$

b. 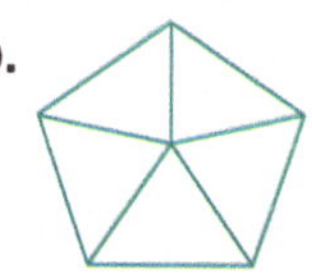

$\frac{3}{5}$

c. 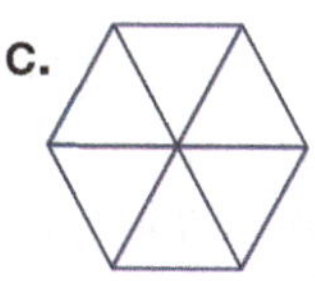

$\frac{5}{6}$

d.

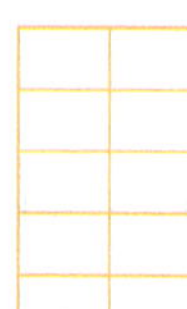

$\frac{7}{10}$

e. 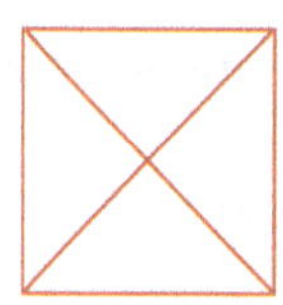

$\frac{3}{4}$

f.

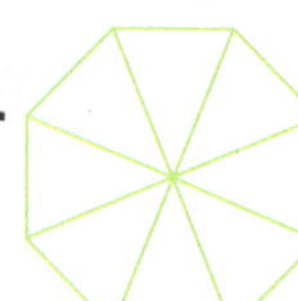

$\frac{3}{8}$

2. Write an equivalent fraction.

a. $\frac{1}{4} = \frac{\square}{8}$ b. $\frac{3}{4} = \frac{\square}{8}$ c. $\frac{2}{5} = \frac{\square}{10}$

3. To add or subtract fractions the denominators MUST be the same. Add or subtract these fractions.

a. $\frac{2}{3} + \frac{1}{6} =$

$\frac{\square}{\square} + \frac{1}{6} = \frac{\square}{\square}$

b. $\frac{5}{8} + \frac{1}{4} =$

$\frac{5}{8} + \frac{\square}{\square} = \frac{\square}{\square}$

The Village of Glen Lea

Read the map and answer the questions below.

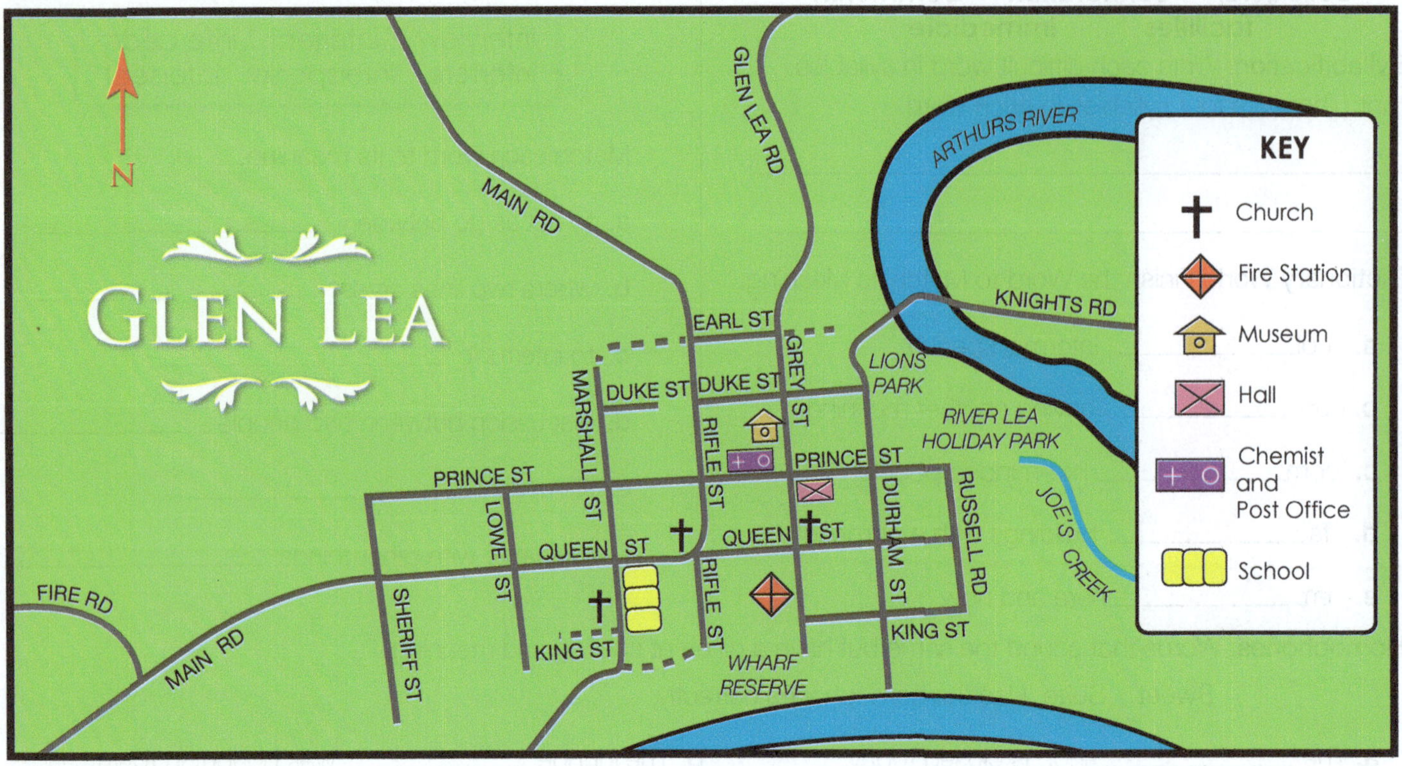

Understanding

Shade the bubble for the best answer.

a. Which of these is closest to the river in Glen Lea?

- ◯ The Holiday Park
- ◯ The Public School
- ◯ The Cemetery
- ◯ The Post Office

b. How many churches are in this village?

- ◯ one
- ◯ two
- ◯ three
- ◯ four

c. Which is the through street in Glen Lea?

- ◯ Queen Street
- ◯ King Street
- ◯ Prince Street
- ◯ Duke Street

d. On which street is the fire station?

- ◯ Marshall
- ◯ Rifle
- ◯ Grey
- ◯ Durham

Interpreting

Write an answer to each question.

a. Which street changes its name twice in the village? ____________________

b. In which direction from the hall is wharf reserve? ____________________

c. On what street is the school situated? ____________________

d. What is on the northern corner of Prince and Grey Streets? ____________________

e. How many people might live in this village? Explain you answer. ____________________

____

Grammar

Adverbial Phrases Adverbs add meaning to nouns – adverbial phrases do not contain a verb.

Underline the adverb in each sentence and write the adverbial phrase on the line.

a. Yesterday, in the rain, we went shopping. ____________________

b. Along the road, Ali and Omar hurried quickly. ____________________

c. Because of the cold, they hurried inside. ____________________

d. Sitting quietly before sunrise you can feel the heat. ____________________

Spelling

Difficult Words to Learn:

beneficial **alternative** **professional** **situation** **entertainment**

Syllabification: Write each word in syllables.

____

____

Alphabetical Order: Write each word in AO.

____

____

Missing Letters: Fill in the missing letters to form a word.

a. ___ e ___ e ___ i ___ i a ___

b. ___ ___ o ___ e ___ ___ i o ___ a ___

c. a ___ ___ e ___ ___ ___ a ___ i ___ e

d. ___ i ___ u a ___ i o ___

Word Building

Adjective to Adverb

Write the adjective from which each adverb is formed.
Eg., quietly is formed from quiet

a. happily ______________

b. possibility ______________

c. grammatically ______________

d. frequently ______________

e. absolutely ______________

f. alternative ______________

Punctuation

The Question Mark ? ? ?

Put a question mark where needed in the following sentences.

a. Is it raining.

b. Come here.

c. How old are you.

d. Well done Omar.

e. Did you say stand still.

f. When is your birthday.

Place Value

1. Round off each number to the nearest **million.**

a. 18 725 816 ______________

b. 72 183 625 ______________

c. 88 598 312 ______________

d. 43 678 298 ______________

2. Identify the place value of each circled numeral.

a. 3 741 625 ______________

b. 7 264 183 ______________

c. 24 689 758 ______________

d. 87 216 385 ______________

3. Write the number showing on each abacus.

a.

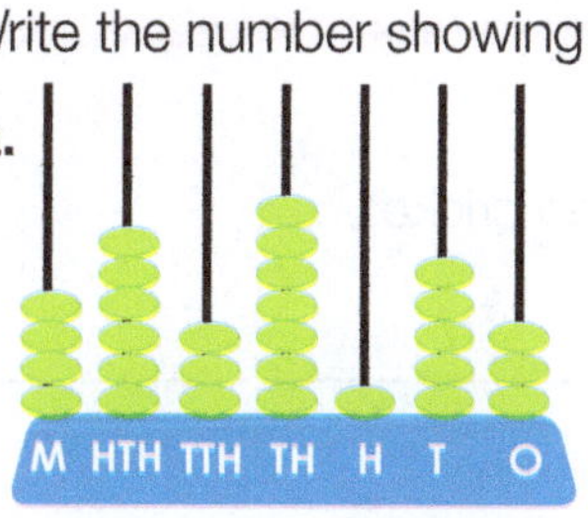

____

b.

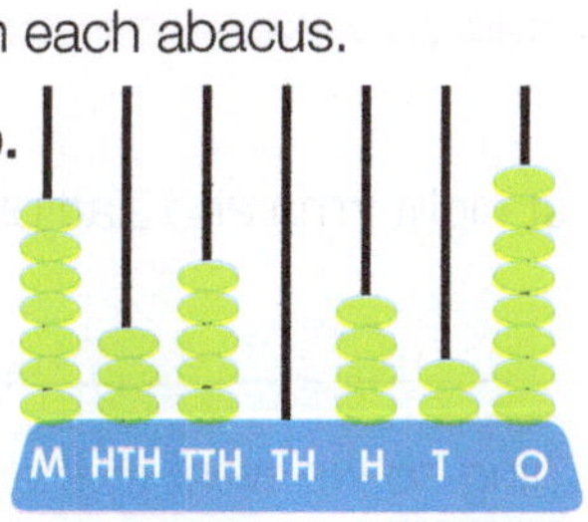

____

Decimal Fractions

1. Write the decimal fraction that falls half-way between each number.

a. 0.6 ______ 0.8

b. 0.25 ______ 0.75

c. 0.68 ______ 0.72

d. 0.85 ______ 0.89

e. 1.75 ______ 2.25

f. 1.336 ______ 1.434

g. 0.883 ______ 1.283

h. 1.825 ______ 1.975

2. Write the decimal fraction for each of these.

a. $\frac{2}{10} =$ ______

b. $\frac{7}{10} =$ ______

c. $\frac{2}{5} =$ ______

d. $\frac{3}{4} =$ ______

e. $\frac{5}{8} =$ ______

f. $1\frac{1}{2} =$ ______

3. Write the place value of each circled number – ones, tenths, hundredths or thousandths.

a. 0.721 ______

b. 2.365 ______

c. 1.752 ______

Explanation

Volcanoes and Earthquakes

Over millions of years boiling hot rocks and gasses bounded around the Sun until they all collected into a ball of liquid rock and formed the Earth. Then over another long period of time the hot, liquid rock cooled down and a hard crust formed around the outside.

The Earth is always changing and as changes happen slowly we don't notice them. However, the Earth's crust can be weakened and broken by the red, hot lava and gasses that break through, spewing out rocks and lava across the land, covering towns and cities in its way. Then the destruction is immense. Volcanic eruptions can also occur under water. When that happens and the red-hot lava cools, a new island may be formed. It is not uncommon for earthquakes to occur in the same parts of the World where there are volcanoes. The rock deep beneath the surface of the Earth moves and then we see splits and cracks happening. These usually happen at weak points, or fault lines, on the Earth's crust.

The epicentre of an earthquake is the point on the Earth's surface directly above where it originates. The magnitude of an earthquake depends on the type of ground where the 'quake hits. For example, the magnitude of 'quakes on soft, sedimentary ground or on mountain tops will be greater than those felt on solid rock. That is why the Newcastle Earthquake caused the buildings to shake violently and collapse in some places and not in others. The most damage was done to buildings that were built on old river sediments. An earthquake is measured on the Richter scale, with the 1989 Newcastle Earthquake measuring 5.6 on that scale.

Landslides can happen because of earthquakes and underwater earthquakes can cause a tsunami. Water can travel across vast areas of oceans creating destructive waves as it gathers speed. Once the water reaches land it can move inland for miles destroying everything in its path. Liquefaction occurs in earthquakes, because beneath the surface is water-saturated sediment, which loses its strength and stiffness during the shaking causing liquid to rise above the ground.

Understanding

Shade the bubble for the best answer.

a. What area of study relates to this subject?
- ◯ biology
- ◯ sociology
- ◯ geology
- ◯ physiology

b. When the earth shakes what causes liquefaction?
- ◯ water-logged soil
- ◯ water-logged sand
- ◯ water-logged rock
- ◯ water-logged islands

c. The strength of an earthquake is also its...?
- ◯ epicentre
- ◯ eruption
- ◯ sediment
- ◯ magnitude

d. Weak parts of the Earth's crust are also called?
- ◯ landslides
- ◯ volcanoes
- ◯ fault lines
- ◯ tsunamis

Interpreting

Tick the box if the information is in the text.

- **a.** The Earth formed from hot rocks and gasses. ☐
- **b.** A volcano is an eruption of hot liquid and gasses. ☐
- **c.** Lava is molten rock issuing from a volcano. ☐
- **d.** An earthquake happens along fault lines. ☐
- **e.** The Richter scale measures earthquakes. ☐
- **f.** Underwater earthquakes cause tsunamis. ☐
- **g.** The Newcastle Earthquake was in 1989. ☐
- **h.** Most damage is done by the water in a tsunami. ☐
- **i.** Earthquake shaking can cause liquefaction. ☐
- **j.** Volcanoes can erupt underwater. ☐

Grammar

Tense – Past, Present and Future

a. Write the following sentence into the present tense. Last night Irma and Zac played cricket.

____

b Write this sentence into the future tense. Today it was raining so we went to the cinema.

____

Spelling

Difficult Words to Learn:

correspondent **dependent** **adolescent** **benevolent** **malevolent**

Change each word from an **adjective** to a **noun**.

____

____

Syllabification: Write the difficult words in syllables.

____

____

Word Meaning: Match the word to its meaning

correspondent **malevolent** **benevolent** **dependent**

a. wishing evil to another ______________________

b. relying upon another ______________________

c. relating one thing to another ______________________

d. doing good for another ______________________

Word Building

Anagrams – Using letters of a word to make another word

Write an anagram for each word.

a. sword ______________________

b. draw ______________________

c. mate ______________________

d. Canberra ______________________

e. Adelaide ______________________

Punctuation

Abbreviations – Used in Sport

Write the meaning of

a. IOC ______________________

b. ICC ______________________

c. NRL ______________________

d. AFL ______________________

e. ARU ______________________

f. NBL ______________________

Factors

1. Write the factors for each number.

a. 16 ☐ ☐ ☐ ☐ and ☐

b. 20 ☐ ☐ ☐ ☐ ☐ and ☐

c.. 12 ☐ ☐ ☐ ☐ ☐ and ☐

d. 18 ☐ ☐ ☐ ☐ ☐ and ☐

2. Circle true T or false F for each factor statement.

a. 7 is a factor of 84. T or F

b. 6 is a factor of 72. T or F

c. 8 is a factor of 48. T or F

d. 9 is a factor of 89. T or F

3. Write the number that has these factors.

a. 1, 2, 3, 4, 6, 9, 12, 18 ________

b. 1, 2, 3, 4, 6, 12, ________

c. 1, 2, 3, 4, 6, 8, 12, 16, 24 ________

d. 1, 2, 3, 5, 6, 10, 15, ________

Addition

1. Circle only the square numbers.

5 10 16 9 18 25

36 84 81 64 9 100

2. Draw a line to match a number to its squared number.

3^2 9 5^2 81 2^2

64

7^2 100 49 4^2 25 8^2

16 4

10^2 9^2 36 6^2

3. Find the difference between squared numbers and composite numbers.

a. $8^2 - 12 =$ ☐ **b.** $7^2 - 9 =$ ☐ **c.** $81 - 5^2 =$ ☐

4. Find the difference between each squared number.

a. $9^2 - 3^2 =$ ☐ **b.** $7^2 - 4^2 =$ ☐ **c.** $6^2 - 2^2 =$ ☐

d. $8^2 - 4^2 =$ ☐ **e.** $8^2 - 6^2 =$ ☐ **f.** $5^2 - 3^2 =$ ☐

Letter to our Local Council

19 August, 2016

Dear Mayor Akram,

The Student Representative Council (SRC) of Smithton Public School would like you to visit our school to discuss the possibility of a marked foot crossing being placed adjacent to our school's front entrance. A large number of students walk to school but they need to cross the road to access the front entrance and at the moment there is no marked safety crossing for them to use.

Recently we had a child suffer a broken leg and severe concussion because he was hit by a motorist who did not stop to allow him to cross the road. This child will be off school for the next six weeks and on crutches for another three to four weeks before he has fully recovered. There have been other incidents where a near miss has occurred and it won't be long before someone is hurt again if we don't get our safety crossing in place soon.

We know you will do everything in your power to help Smithton PS and we would like the opportunity to meet and outline where the crossing can be best situated. We want to impress on you the immediate need to resolve this matter in order to keep our students safe.

We look forward to your visit so we can discuss this matter with you in more detail.

Yours sincerely,

Assef Khan. SRC Rep.

Understanding

Circle **T** (True) of **F** (False) to answer correctly

a. The school would like a marked crossing for safety reasons. **T** **F**

b. There has already been an accident in front of the school **T** **F**

c. The mayor is being lobbied by the school for a marked crossing. **T** **F**

d. The crossing should go behind the school's front gate. **T** **F**

Interpreting

Write an answer to each question.

a. Why do the school students want a marked foot crossing? ______________________

____

b. Who has written the letter to the mayor? ______________________

____

c. Why do the students want to talk personally to the mayor? ______________________

____

d. What is the imperative expressed in the letter? ______________________

____

e. How dangerous is the area for the students? ______________________

____

Grammar

Adjectival Clauses Adjectival clauses contain verbs and begin with relative pronouns – **whose, whom, who, which** or **that**. Underline the adjectival clauses in each sentence.

a. The mayor, who is very busy, will visit soon.

b. Our school, which needs a safe crossing, is closed.

c. The SRC, whose job it is to help us, works well.

d. Do you know the boy who broke his leg?

e. The crossing that we need is important.

f. Assef Khan, to whom we spoke, represents us.

Spelling

Difficult Words to Learn:

accommodate **necessity** **continuous** **competitive** **eventual**

Syllabification: Write the words in syllables

____

____

Proof Reading: Circle the errors and write the words correctly on the line

a. The major and his consil will discuss the isue at there next meeting.

____

____

b. Wen will your be able to accomodate our class at yore resaut?

____

____

Word Building

Of - Off or From??

Examples of Use: Take this **from** me.

Get it **off** me now! They are two **of** a kind.

Use the correct word in each sentence.

a. There are many _______ those apricots on our fruit trees.

b. Make sure you get it _______ him today.

c. They went _______ together to get as many _______ the boxes _______ the man as they could carry.

Punctuation

The Exclamation Mark. ! ! ! Show the exclamation mark correctly in these sentences.

a. Jump now
b. Don't do that
c. Can you stop that please
d. I am not going I said
e. Not good Ali
f. Play the ball skipper
g. Will you go
h. It's not right I tell you
i. That's the house, the one on the hill

Transformation

1. **Reflect**, **translate** or **rotate** each shape.

a. 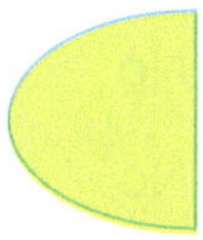 REFLECT →

b.  ROTATE →

c. 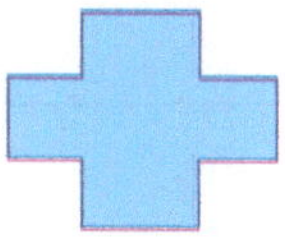 TRANSLATE →

2. Use **reflection** to draw the other half of the numeral or letter.

a. 

b. 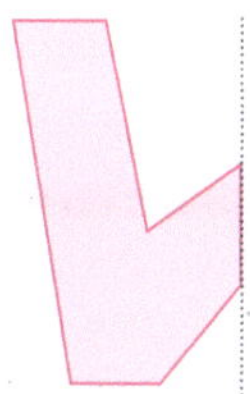

c. 

d. 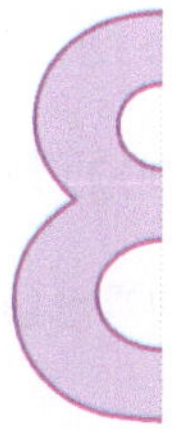

Chance

1. Write the possibility for each circumstance, as a fraction.

a. Toss a head with a coin.

b. Roll an odd number with a die.

c. Toss two heads with three coins.

2. Write the possible outcome for each as a percentage.

a. land on red **b.** land on 10 **c.** land on 12

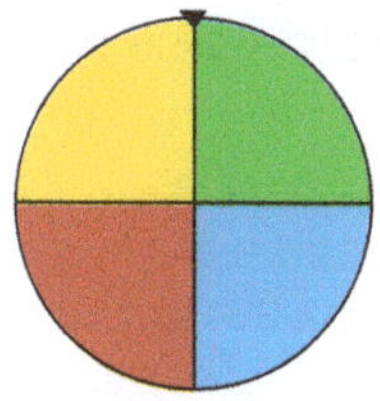

_______ % _______ % _______ %

3. Here is a 'feely bag' with ten discs. Write the chance of drawing the colours as a percentage.

a. red _______ % **b.** blue _______ %

c. green _______ %

d. yellow_______ %

Using Digital Devices in the Classroom

We all know the term BYOD. Some of us know it too well because we forgot to bring one with us to school and our teacher was none-too-happy with us for forgetting it. After all, the day we had to bring it with us was the day we were to sit the new, on-line English tests. We were supposed to have our own device so we could use it to do a writing test and it was supposed to be fully charged and ready to go for the whole day.

Now just what is the device we could use? Well, it could be a laptop, a notebook, a tablet or a PC but it could not be a mobile 'phone. These devices can be run using a plug-in power pack and need to be fully charged to allow all-day, classroom use. Of course the one big problem, that can make things difficult, is if all of them don't have the same operating system. Then it could be impossible to access on-line sites and programs that sit on a different platform.

When doing a spelling or writing test you will have to close any spell checker you have running. Do you know how to do that? When using your own device for a writing test you will need to have a good understanding of how a word processor works, particularly when you come to editing your work. It would be terrible if you went to change something only to find you are deleting a lot of text and don't know why. Can you think of what could be making all your text disappear? Well, that is something you will need to learn.

Does this make sense to you or do you find it difficult to understand digital terminology? Perhaps you can improve your knowledge by finding the meaning of some of the terms in this unit.

Understanding

Circle **Yes** or **No** to answer each question.

a. Is it easy to use your own device for schoolwork? Yes No

b. Can you use a mobile 'phone for the English tests? Yes No

c. Should spell check be turned off for a spelling test? Yes No

d. Can a device be charged for all-day use? Yes No

e. Is knowledge of word processing important when editing? Yes No

Interpreting

Write an answer to each question.

a. What does BYOD mean? ______________________________

b. What might need to be checked if text disappears when editing? ______________________________

c. What is the most common operating system on a PC? ______________________________

d. What is a PC? ______________________________

e. Which device would you prefer to use and why? ______________________________

Grammar

Adjectives – this or that – these or those

Cross out the incorrect adjective in each sentence.

a. (Those / This) book belongs to him.

b. Can you give him (that / these) shoes please?

c. From now on (that / those) gates will be shut.

d. Before too long (these / this) flowers will bloom.

e. The cricket ball and (this / these) bat will do.

f. Buy (this / those) games for his birthday.

Spelling

Difficult Words to Learn:

alcohol **vehicle** **chocolate** **Christmas** **lightning**

Alphabetical Order: Write the words in AO.

____

____

Dictionary Practice: Write the word that comes first in the dictionary?

a. algorithm, alcohol ______________

b. Christmas, Christians ______________

c. lightning, lighten ______________

d. Islam, Islamic ______________

e. vehicular, vehicle ______________

Word Building

Using the **Prefix 'off'** with the **Hyphen**

Write another new word using 'off' with the hyphen

Eg. off-beat

a. colour ______________ **b.** spring ______________

c. side ______________ **d.** peak ______________

e. chance ______________ **f.** season ______________

g. cut ______________ **h.** shoot ______________

i. sider ______________ **j.** putting ______________

k. hand ______________ **l.** beat ______________

Common Errors: Words to Learn – Use **Mnemonics**

a. occasion (Don't make an **ass** of yourself!)

b. receive ('I' before 'e' except after 'c')

c. stationery ('er' for paper)

d. stationary ('ar' for a parked car)

Punctuation

Abbreviations – in Technology

Write the meaning of

a. USB ______________________________ **b.** RAM ______________________________

c. wp ______________________________ **d.** db ______________________________

e. www ______________________________ **f.** ROM ______________________________

Area

1. Calculate the area of each shape. Divide each shape into rectangles and apply the formula length x width (breadth) L X W = Area.

a.

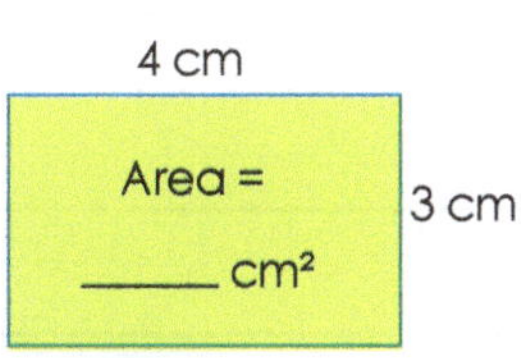

b.

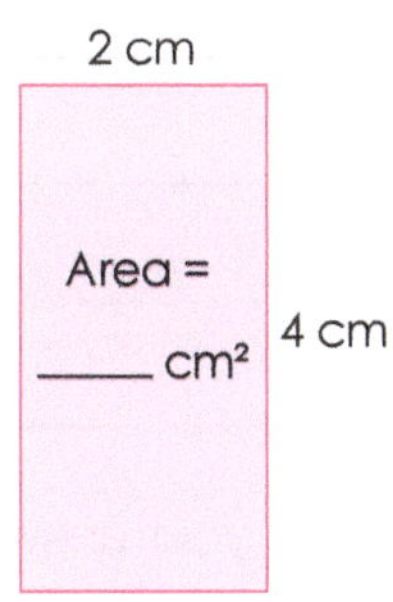

c.

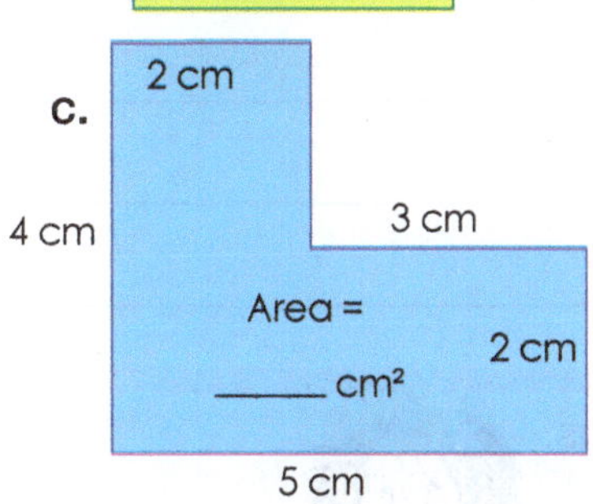

d.

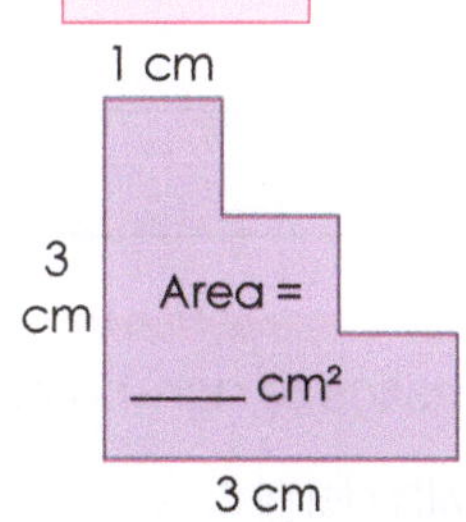

2. To find the area of a triangle multiply height x ½ base. Find the area of each triangle. (Don't forget the unit of area = cm².)

a. Area = ______________

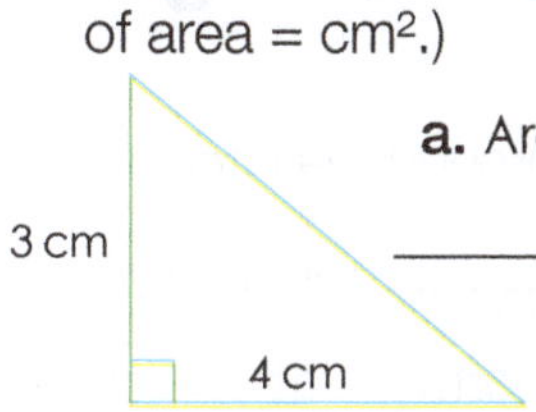

b. Area = ______________

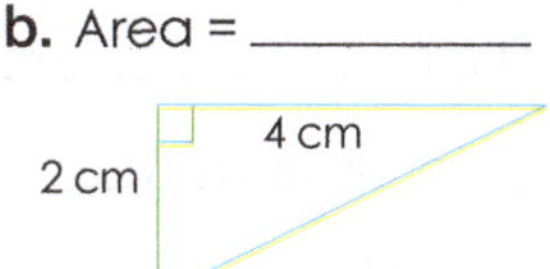

Data

The data shows tidal movements over one week. The table shows the high and low tides.

Days	Sun	Mon	Tues	Wed	Thurs	Fri	Sat
High Tide	1.8m	2.1m	1.9m	1.7m	1.8m	2.3m	1.95m
Low Tide	0.2m	0.3m	0.4m	0.1m	0.5m	0.7m	0.0m

1. Dot plot the above data on this graph and join the dots to make a two line graph. Show high tides in blue and low tides in red.

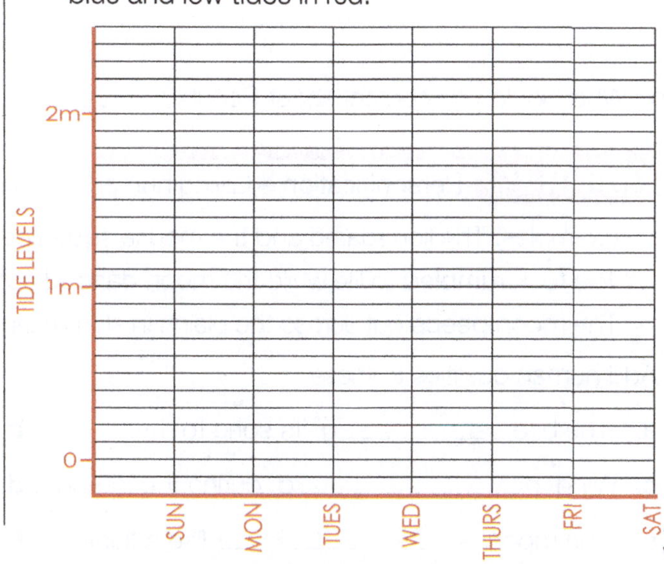

The Monthly Rag - Contents Page

Understanding

Circle **Yes** or **No** to answer each question.

a. Is there someone listed as a contact for the markets? Yes No

b. Does the Monthly Rag have an editor? Yes No

c. Are children catered for in this publication? Yes No

d. Is there anything of interest to you in The Rag? Yes No

e. Do the sporting events indicate what time of the year it might be? Yes No

Interpreting

Write an answer to each question.

a. Explain what "Barbies Galore" means? ______________________

b. What would you buy from the Market Growers Markets? ______________________

c. Is this publication for a large town? Explain your answer. ______________________

____

d. Who do you think this "Rag" might interest the most? Explain your answer. ______________________

____

e. Who would you contact about Scouts? ______________________

Grammar

Personification – Giving human characteristics to non-human things.

Examples: The lion **roared** and the mouse **squealed** with delight.

The rock **rumbled** to life while the moon **danced** across the waves.

The moon **peeps** out across the plains in shimmering, silver shards of light.

Add human qualities to these

a. The bird ___ ___ ___ g its song to me.

b. Fire h ___ ___ ___ r ___ ___ d around the kitchen.

c. Wind h ___ ___ ___ ___ d, during the tornado.

d. Octopus arms gr ___ ___ ___ ___ ___ me tightly.

e. The moon s ___ ___ ___ k ___ like a thief.

f. The ship g ___ ___ d ___ d into port.

Spelling

Difficult Words to Learn:

ubiquitous liquefy brusque acquaint colloquial

Alphabetical Order: Write the words in AO.

____

____

Note: 'q' is followed by 'u' except in QANTAS which is an acronym

Write ten words that have a 'qu' combination: Eg. queen

____

____

Missing Letters: Fill in the missing letters to form a difficult word.

a. u __ i q __ __ t __ __ s **b.** b r __ s q __ __

c. __ o __ __ o q __ __ __ l **d.** __ c q __ a i __ t

Word Building

'ck' Words with the sound of 'k"Eg., suck

Add consonants to form words with the sound of 'k'.

a. __ __ u __ __

b. __ a __ __

c. __ a __ __ e __

d. __ __ i __ __ e __

e. __ __ a __ __ e __

f. __ __ e __ __ e __

Punctuation

Punctuation: The Hyphen and Numbers - Eg., twenty-one, ninety-nine, one-third

Write the following correctly on the line.

a. two thirds ______________ **b.** twenty seven ______________

c. one half ______________ **d.** three and one quarter ______________

Volume and Capacity

1. Remember, one litre of water will balance a one kilogram mass. Write the mass of each measure of water.

a. 250mL = ______g **b.** 700mL = ______g

c. 1000mL = ______g **d.** 1500mL = ______g

e. 550mL = ______g **f.** $8\frac{1}{2}$ Litres = ______g

2. Write each capacity as a decimal.

a. 3750mL = ______ L **b.** 2250mL = ______ L

c. 1050mL = ______ L **d.** 350mL = ______ L

e. 9483mL = ______ L **f.** 795 mL = ______ L

3. Find the volume of each object. (One block = 10 grams)

a.

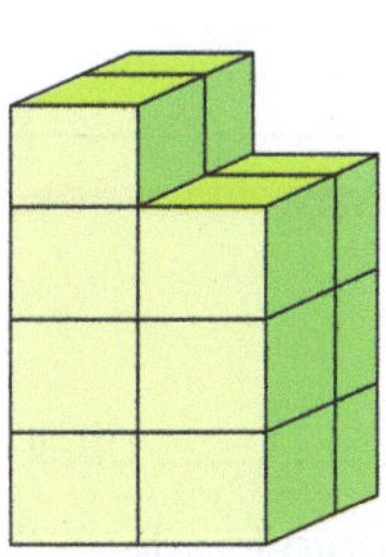

Volume =______ g

b.

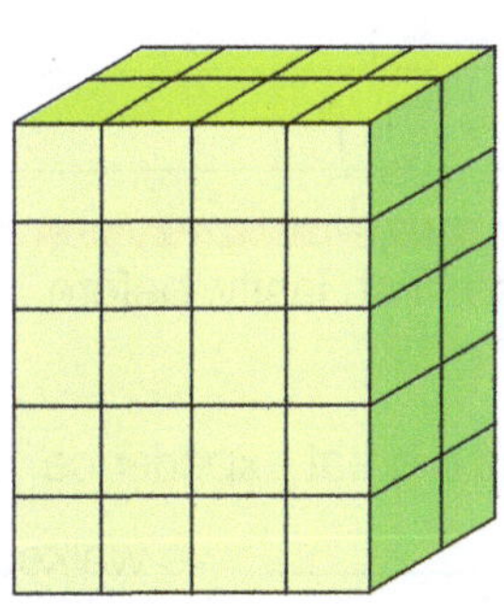

Volume =______ g

Number Patterns

1. Fill in the missing numbers in each group.
Look for the pattern.

a.	7	11	13	17			
b.	4	9	16	25			
c.	1	3	6	10			

2. Apply the rule in the centre to the adjacent number and finish the number wheels.

a.

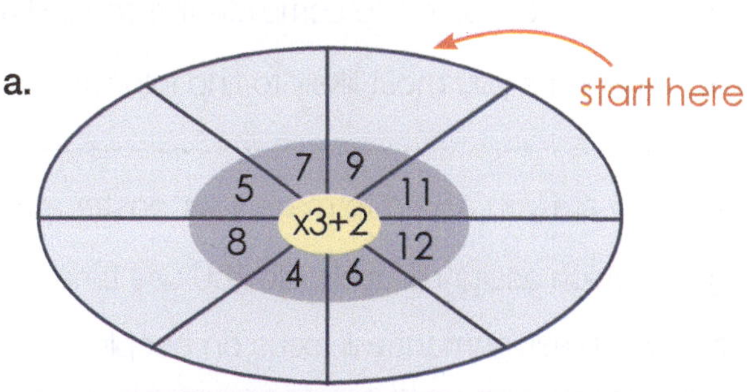

b.

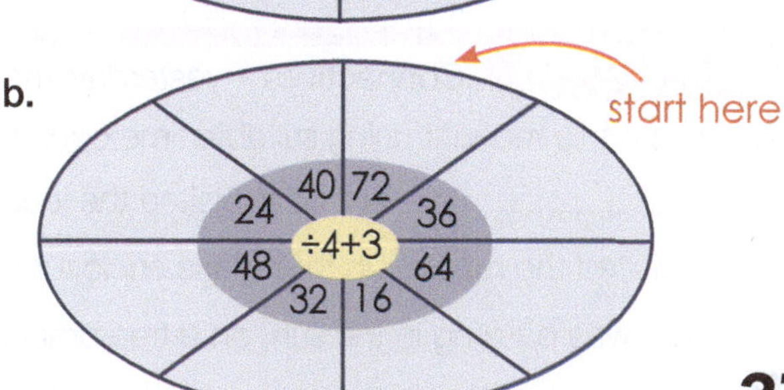

Writing Tasks for Term Three

Your teacher has prepared this hand-out for your information. Its purpose is to assist you in planning and writing your Term Three English tasks. Use it to guide you when completing each task.

Narrative

July 30
Due in by Aug 15

Get ready to write the most outlandish and exciting story you can think of. Make sure it has an **orientation** that gets your readers immediate attention. You should also think about the **plot** and how you can weave a **complication** into your writing. Remember to use **short paragraphs** that begin with a **topic sentence** and use lots of **action verbs** as well as **thinking and feeling verbs** too. A little bit of **dialogue** is OK to keep your story alive and energetic but don't over-do it. Plan the most exciting part or **climax** of the story and provide a great **resolution** for the complication. You might also like to add a final **comment** to finish off the story.

Factual Recount

August 20
Due in August 31

Topic: *Migration in Australia After World War 1*
Remember to **research** the details and events that happened during this migration period. A factual recount is about historical events. In your **opening statement** you need to cover the **who, when and where** of migration and use **proper nouns and pronouns** as well as **time connectives** in your **paragraphs**. This will help you arrange the **order of events** and **comments** on migration too. Finish with a **concluding statement** about this historical time in Australia's history.

Visual Text

Sept. 4
Due in by
End of Term

Advertisement: *The School Sport's Day*
Design a poster for the up-coming School Sport's Day in Term Four. Make it as **attractive and informative** as you can to entice as many parents and friends to attend the day. You should identify all the **attractions and events** being held on that day and put the **time** the day will begin and end. If there will be **refreshments** available, don't forget to include each **item and its cost**. Your poster will be **judged** on: Its visual appeal and Its content, including its informative details. The **best judged poster** by the principal will be used to promote the day.

Understanding and Interpreting

Write an answer to each question.

a. What is the purpose of this hand-out? ____________________

b. What are the basic elements of a narrative? ____________________

____

c. Who will judge the advertisement? ____________________

d. What must you do to complete the second assignment? ____________________

e. Where are you most likely to find information on migration to Australia? ____________________

____

f. Why are you asked to make your poster attractive and informative? ____________________

g. In which assignment should you use time connectives? ____________________

h. Which assignment will focus on people? ____________________

Grammar

Connectives – yesterday, then, afterwards, first, lastly, before …

Complete this recount using suitable time connectives.

__________ our class visited the local zoo. It was a great experience. __________ of all we visited the reptiles, in their glass enclosure. __________ we walked along the path to where the Koala was basking in the sun, on a tree branch. __________ we feed the monkeys and had lunch __________ visiting the elephants and cheetahs.

Spelling

More Difficult Words to Learn:

abbreviate **interrogate** **concrete**
celebrate **motivate**

Syllabification: Write each word in syllables.

____

____

Change each word to a participle by adding 'ing' but remember to drop the 'e' at the end.

____

____

Word Building

Compound Words – Use: **swim, keeper, goal, suit, wealth, common,** to make a compound word.

a. ______________________

b. ______________________

c. ______________________

Dictionary Practice: Find the meaning of these words in the dictionary.

a. interrogate **b.** motivate

______________________ ______________________

Correct the underlined words. Write each word correctly on the line.

a. Omar and Samir <u>was</u> having a <u>brthday</u> <u>partie</u>. ______________________

b. Ian and Lou <u>bout</u> a <u>knew</u> boat on <u>Wenesdsay</u>. ______________________

Punctuation

Shortened Words Write the abbreviation for each word or phrase.

a. word processor ________ **b.** data base ________ **c.** Excel ________

d. Electronic mail ________ **e.** digital video data ________ **f.** multi-media ________

Fractions

1. Write either 'prime' or 'composite' for each number.

a. 7 ________ **b.** 9 ________

c. 8 ________ **d.** 11 ________

e. 21 ________ **f.** 23 ________

g. 39 ________ **h.** 51 ________

2. Circle the numbers that can be divided by each factor.

a. 2 7, 9, 4, 12, 27, 34

b. 3 7, 9, 4, 12, 27, 34

c. 5 6, 10, 17, 25, 38, 75

3. Write the prime factors for these.

a. 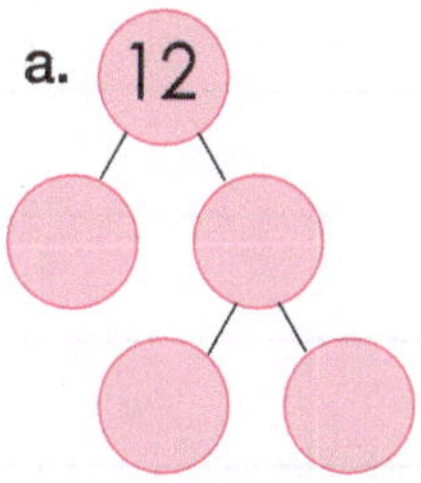

b. 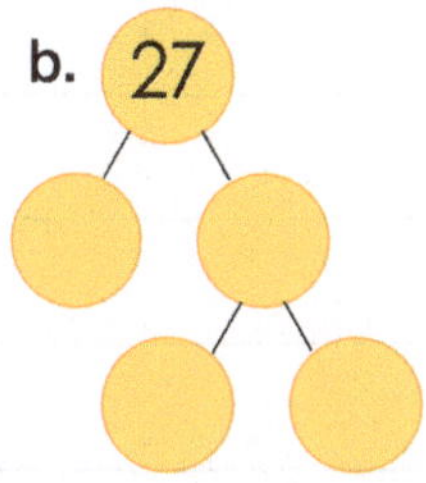

c. 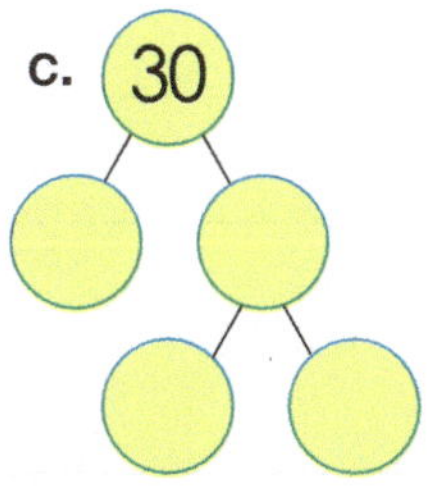

Fractions

1. Write each fraction in its lowest form.

a. $\frac{14}{21} = \square$ **b.** $\frac{8}{12} = \square$ **c.** $\frac{9}{27} = \square$

d. $\frac{8}{10} = \square$ **e.** $\frac{6}{10} = \square$ **f.** $\frac{10}{20} = \square$

2. Change the improper fraction to a mixed number fraction. Divide the denominator into the numerator.

$\frac{8}{5} = 1\frac{3}{5}$ **a.** $\frac{11}{5} =$ ______ **b.** $\frac{11}{8} =$ ______

c. $\frac{5}{2} =$ ______ **d.** $\frac{9}{7} =$ ______ **e.** $\frac{5}{4} =$ ______

f. $\frac{12}{5} =$ ______ **g.** $\frac{7}{3} =$ ______ **h.** $\frac{12}{10} =$ ______

3. Write each fraction as a percentage.

a. $\frac{1}{5} =$ ____% **b.** $\frac{3}{4} =$ ____% **c.** $\frac{3}{10} =$ ____%

d. $\frac{1}{2} =$ ____% **e.** $\frac{4}{5} =$ ____%

Rip Van Winkle

Once upon a time in a mountain town of Sleepy Hollow, men would gather at evening time to tell tales of intrigue and magic about the mountains surrounding their home. One of those men was Rip Van Winkle. Now his tale was about a group of tiny men he came across one day when he went to cut timber in the forest. The men had long white beards and they were seen playing a game of nine pins. That game can be likened to our game of ten pin bowling. They invited Rip Van Winkle to play with them and he did.

While he waited his turn to bowl he joined the men in drinking from the wooden cask they had with them. But soon he became sleepy and was unable to stay awake. When Rip Van Winkle finally did wake up he was astonished to find his clothes had become old rags, his gun was rusty and useless, his dog was gone and he had grown a long, white beard which almost reached the ground. Of course the little old men he had been drinking with were nowhere to be seen. This puzzled him and so he returned home only to find his young son was now a big man and all the village folk he once knew had died or had grown old too. Then Rip Van Winkle realised he had been asleep for twenty years.

Now even though he searched for those tiny men he never found them but every time the sound of thunder echoed through the valley it reminded him of the sound the nine pins made when he was playing with the tiny men all those years ago. So he believed those tiny men were there, hiding away somewhere in the mountains, but he never saw them again.

Understanding

Shade the bubble for the best answer.

a. Which title would best suit this tale?
- ◯ Sleepy Hollow
- ◯ Nine Pin Bowling
- ◯ The Curse of Sleepy Hollow
- ◯ The Man Who Slept for Twenty Years

b. What was Rip Van Winkle's occupation?
- ◯ a story teller
- ◯ a forestry worker
- ◯ a forestry ranger
- ◯ a lumber jack

c. Which word relates best to the 'tiny men'?
- ◯ goblins
- ◯ wizards
- ◯ dwarfs
- ◯ gnomes

d. Which best describes the cask's contents?
- ◯ potion
- ◯ wine
- ◯ spirits
- ◯ beer

Interpreting

Circle **Yes** or **No** to answer each question.

a. The tiny men were real people.	Yes	No
b. Rip Van Winkle was a real person.	Yes	No
c. All of Rip Van Winkle's friends had died.	Yes	No
d. Rip Van Winkle had a son.	Yes	No
e. The story is set in a mountain town.	Yes	No
f. Sleepy Hollow inhabitants were storytellers.	Yes	No

Grammar

Complex Verbs Example: Rip Van Winkle was hoping to find the little men.

Underline the complex verbs in each sentence. Write the verbs on the line.

a. He waited, turned to bowl and missed the pins. ________________

b. They were singing and dancing to enjoy their party. ________________

c. Don't go there to get your vegetables. ________________

d. Everyone was trying to lift the car off the baby. ________________

e. He tried to help carry the baby to safety. ________________

Spelling

More Difficult Words to Learn:

edible **available** **responsive**
questionable **valuable**

Antonyms: Re-write each word using the prefix **'un'** or **'in'** to form opposites.

____

____

Homophones: prey, preyed, pray, prayed

Use each word correctly in the sentence.

a. The eagle is a large bird of ____________.

b. We ____________ for rain to break the drought.

c. The people ____________ for those who were killed.

d. The fox ____________ on the chickens.

Word Building

Prefix 'anti' or 'ante'

Add the prefix 'anti' or 'ante' to make a new word. Write the new word.

a. clockwise ____________

b. room ____________

c. septic ____________

d. meridian ____________

e. venom ____________

f. social ____________

Plurals: Some Plurals Change the Base Word. Write each word in the plural.

a. mouse ____________ **b.** tooth ____________ **c.** woman ____________

d. foot ____________ **e.** child ____________ **f.** goose ____________

Some words do not change. sheep, fish, deer, trout, salmon, bream scissors, trousers …

Punctuation

The Dash – A break or a Pause Note the use of the dash in this sentence.

We broke for lunch – then resumed at 2:00pm. Note the position when used to show the omission of letters in words: R _ _ V _ _ W _ _ k _ _.

Place Value

1. Write the number showing on the abacus by the counters.

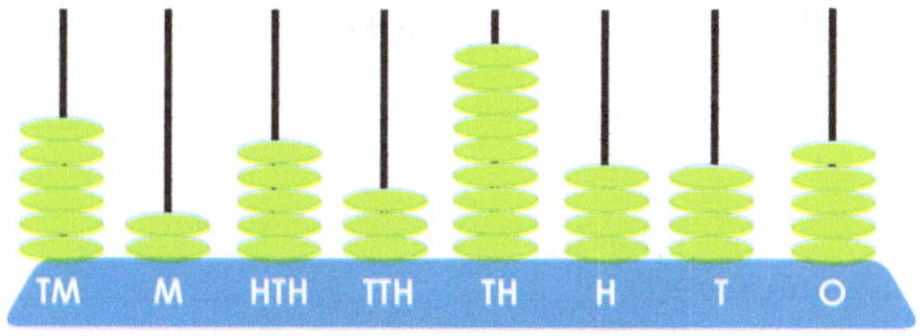

2. Arrange 4,9,6,3,2,8,7,1,4 to make the **largest** possible number.

3. How many millions in 48 326 172?

4. Round off 38 716 214 to the nearest million.

5. 30 000 000 + 8 000 000 + 200 000 + 40 000 + 7 000 + 900 + 60 + 4 =

Arrange each set of numbers in **ascending** order

6. 38 217 430, 18 516 210, 49 324 788, 23 417 602

____

Addition

1. Find the total for each algorithm.

a.

	TTH	TH	H	T	U
	8	3	6	4	1
		3	2	8	7
+		5	1	0	2

b.

	TTH	TH	H	T	U
	1	5	3	2	7
	3	2	8	9	1
+			4	3	8

c.

	TTH	TH	H	T	U
	5	4	3	0	4
		3	2	8	4
+		2	8	5	6

d.

	TTH	TH	H	T	U
	6	4	1	3	2
	2	8	4	1	3
+		2	8	5	4

2. Add each sum of money.

a.
$2713.54
1690.38
+2683.09
$.

b.
$4712.55
2007.93
+6985.02
$.

3. Use a calculator to add the group of numbers.

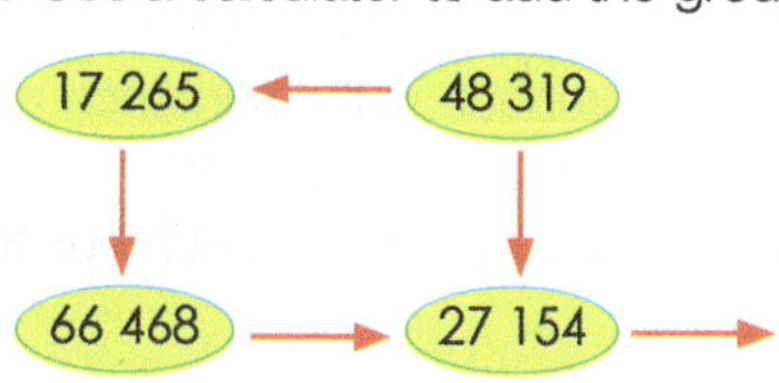

TOTAL ____________

Should there be a Year 6 Farewell Dinner?

Here are a few of the responses to this question. They are representative of most student responses.

Taylor
Head Prefect
I think we should have a farewell dinner because it will be the last opportunity for us all to be together and share a meal before we go our separate ways in high school.

Jorja
SRC Rep.
Having a farewell dinner gives us all an opportunity to make speeches, wish each other the best of luck at high school and to thank our teachers and parents for helping us throughout our years at primary school.

Dean
Student
It will be sad if we don't have our farewell dinner. My sister had one when she was in Year 6 and I think Year 6 students look forward to having a party to say good-bye and celebrate their seven years of schooling.

Josh
Student
Maybe we could put the money we would spend on having a dinner towards something for the school. This might be a good way for everyone to remember us and for us to say 'thank you' to our school.

Ari
Student
This is a big decision for us to make. Can everyone afford to pay for the cost of a farewell dinner? If someone will miss out coming because they do not have the money to pay then maybe we don't have one.

The SRC had the job of looking at the responses and coming up with an answer to suit everyone.

Understanding

Shade the bubble for the best answer.

a. Whose response values friendship?
○ Taylor ○ Jorja
○ Ari ○ Josh

b. Which student likes a party?
○ Jorja ○ Dean
○ Ari ○ Josh

c. Whose response shows thoughtfulness?
○ Jorja ○ Dean
○ Ari ○ Josh

d. Which response is the most altruistic?
○ Taylor ○ Dean
○ Ari ○ Josh

Interpreting

Write an answer to each question.

a. Which word or phrase means this is a sample of the responses received? ______________________

b. What decision would you make given the responses? ______________________

c. Why would it be sad not to have the dinner? ______________________

d. How important are Ari's concerns? ______________________

e. Why are there more responses just from students? ______________________

Grammar

Cohesive Links – Possessive Pronouns – mine, yours, his, hers, ours, theirs

Underline the possessive pronouns in each sentence.

a. His mother is mine and yours too.

b. That is our dog and the horses are also ours.

c. "Which one is yours?" asked his mum.

d. "This one is mine," replied his sister.

Use a correct possessive pronoun in the sentence.

e. When it was ______________ turn to bat he used ______________ new one.

Spelling

More Difficult Words to Learn:

demonstrate **hesitate** **concentrate** **situate** **educate**

Nominalisation: Write the difficult words as Nouns

____

____

Word Meaning: Match each word to its meaning.

a. to hold back ______________

b. to show how it's done ______________

c. to develop the mind ______________

d. to locate at a site ______________

Dictionary Practice: Write the word that comes last in the dictionary in each group

a. demons, demonstrate ______________

b. hesitation, hemisphere ______________

c. countenance, countersign ______________

d. slice, slick ______________

Word Building

Prefixes – Almost always followed by a Hyphen.

Prefixes: all non ex half self

Use a prefix with each word. Eg., all –rounder

a. important ______________

b. electric ______________

c. event ______________

d. smoking ______________

e. convict ______________

f. serviceman ______________

g. hourly ______________

h. back ______________

i. made ______________

Punctuation

Using **Articles – a, an, the** Complete each sentence using the correct article.

a. Can you buy me ______ apple and ______ orange at ______ shop please?

b. He has ______ car but it is at ______ garage being fixed so he needs ______ loan of yours.

c. When we had ______ cat and ______ dog we found it hard to leave ______ gate open for them.

Integers

1. Show each number sentence on the number line. Write the result.

a. - 3 + 2 - 6 + 5 - 1 = ☐

b. - 4 + 5 + 4 - 3 = ☐

2. Write each group of numbers in **ascending** order.

a. -2, +3, -5, -3, +2, 0, -4, +4

____

b. +6, -4, +2, +3, -3, -2, 0, +1

____

3. Complete each number sentence. Some will have negative answers.

a. + 3 - 7 = ☐ **b.** - 5 + 9 = ☐ **c.** - 6 + 4= ☐

Two-digit Multiplication

1. Find the product of each algorithm. Use the extended form of multiplication. One is done for you.

a.
```
    623
  x  27
 +1 +2
   4361
+ 12460   Add a zero
  16821
```

b.
```
    325
  x  35
```

c.
```
    472
  x  43
```

2. PROBLEMS

a. There are 64 pieces of liquorice in a bag. How many pieces in 37 bags?

x ______

______ pieces

b. 48 rows seat 52 people in a movie theatre. How many seats in the theatre?

x ______

______ seats

Internet (On-Line) Shopping

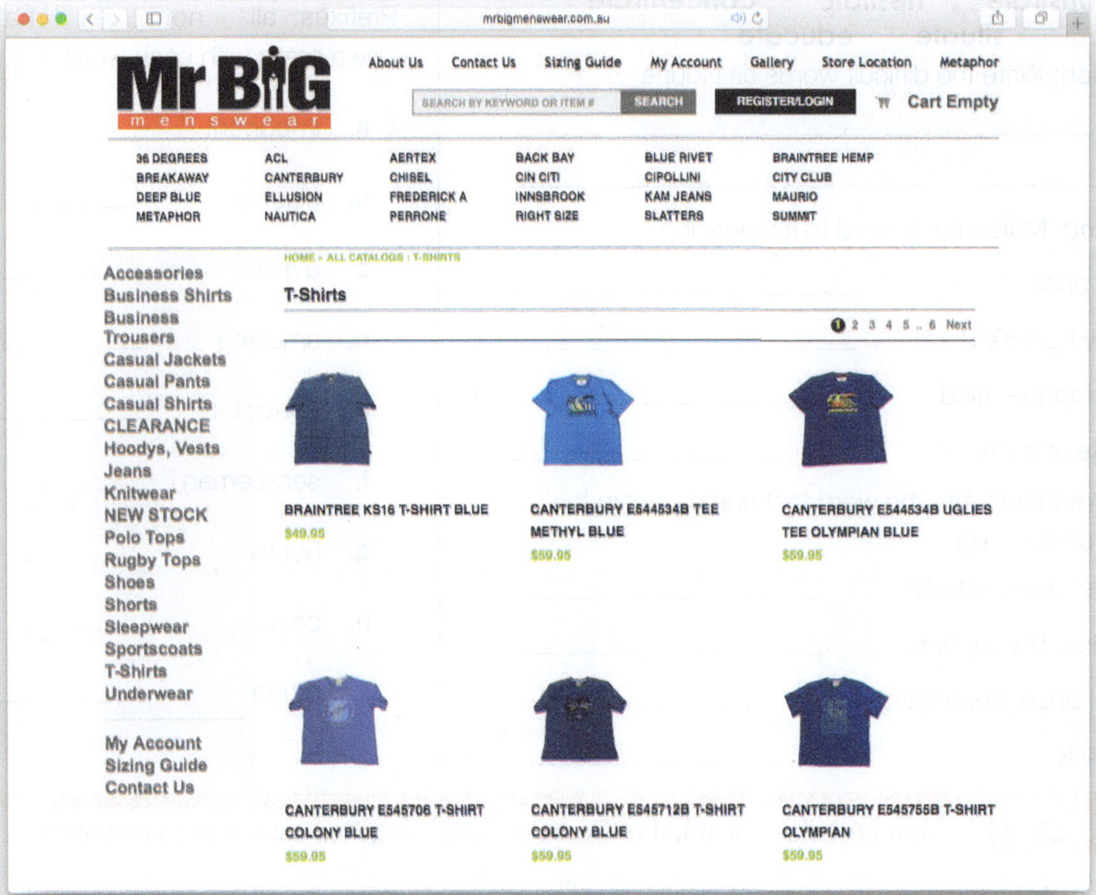

Understanding

Circle **Yes** or **No** to answer the question.

a. Is this a true web site?	Yes	No	
b. Is this an Australian web site?	Yes	No	
c. Are there a lot of T-Shirts for sale?	Yes	No	
d. Can you buy items on this site?	Yes	No	
e. Does this store have sale items?	Yes	No	
f. Is the logo self-explanatory?	Yes	No	
g. Are goods listed in AO?	Yes	No	
h. Would the T-Shirts fit everyone?	Yes	No	
i. Is on-line shopping convenient?	Yes	No	
j. Is this the store's Home Page?	Yes	No	

Interpreting

Write an answer to each question.

a. What is the address of this web site? ______________________________

b. Where would you look to check your size? ______________________________

c. How could you find the clearance items? ______________________________

d. Where is Mr Big Menswear Store located? ______________________________

e. How would you pay for your on-line shopping? ______________________________

Grammar

Compound Verbs A Helper and a Main Verb

Example: He **has worried** about the outcome of his test for days. Underline the compound verbs in each sentence.

a. We have rung the shop to find out when it will be open.

b. He has seen the doctor today.

c. We have been lucky with our new X-Box.

d. They had been told there could be trouble soon.

e. Can you imagine how far he has come!

f. The children have done all the work between them.

Spelling

Unit 21

More Difficult Words to Learn:

extravagant **arrogant** **significant**
tolerant **brilliant**

Change each word from an adjective to a noun ending in 'ance'.

____

____

Proof Reading: Write each word correctly

a. mistery ________ **b.** beried ________

c. proply ________ **d.** ocassion ________

e. ninty nine ________ **f.** scisors ________

g. butiful ________ **h.** exploshuns ________

i. sunamie ________

Missing Letters: Fill in the missing consonants

a. __ i __ __ i __ i __ a __ __ **b.** __ o __ e __ a __ __

c. __ __ i __ __ i a __ __ **d.** a __ __ o __ a __ __

Word Building

Suffixes – When adding 'full' as a suffix drop the last 'l'

Write each word with 'full' as a suffix.

a. play ________

b. help ________

c. thought ________

d. wonder ________

e. thank ________

f. resource ________

g. forget ________

h. use ________

i. spoon ________

Punctuation

Capital Letter for Personal Pronoun "I" and Christian Names.

Re-write each sentence using the correct punctuation.

a. when i went to see omar and mustafa at bankstown i caught the bus to roselands first

____

b. you and i could go with mark and ari to see the new star wars show on Saturday

____

Division

1. Complete each division. Write the remainder as a fraction.

a. 5)517 r ___ **b.** 4)825 r ___ **c.** 3)637 r ___

d. 7)841 r ___ **e.** 2)735 r ___ **f.** 6)715 r ___

2. a. If I earn $180 in 6 hours how much do I earn per hour? $ ________

b. Joshua rides 210 kilometres each week. How far does he ride each day? ________

3. Complete each division. Write the remainder as a decimal.

a. 4)2353.0 **b.** 5)5372.0

c. 2)3751.0 **d.** 10)3052.0

Time

1. Write the pm time on each clock face in 24 hour time.

a. 

b. 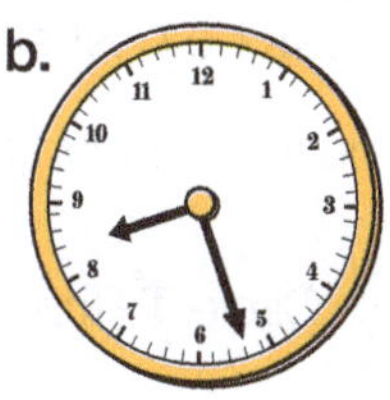

c. 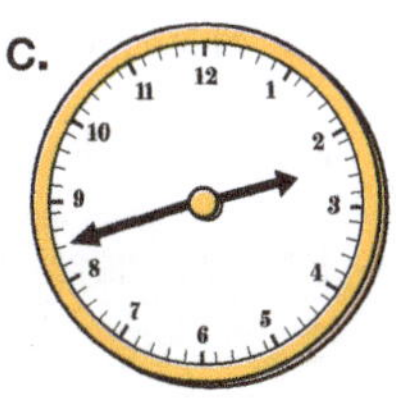

2. Write the 24 hour time in am or pm time.

a. 23:45 = ________ **b.** 07:30 = ________

c. 21:36 = ________ **d.** 15:50 = ________

3. Calculate the time lapse between each given time.

a. 07:15 till 3:50pm ________

b. 13:45 till 18:37 ________

c. 8:30am Tuesday till 13:25 the next day ________

These poems are humorous and fun to read. With five lines in total, lines one, two and five rhyme with each other and lines three and four rhyme with each other. Sometimes lines one and five end in the same word.

The typical ***rhythm*** of a limerick is:

bah-DAH, bah-bah-DAH, bah-bah-DAH,
bah-DAH, bah-bah-DAH, bah-bah-DAH
bah-DAH, bah-bah-DAH
bah-DAH, bah-bah-DAH
bah-DAH, bah-bah-DAH, bah-bah-DAH

An example-

Here sits an old man from the west
Who has by his side the very best
No doubt he will find
The drink is divine
If ever he has time for the rest

Try some limericks of your own. Use these first lines to get started. Write some rhyming words first.

There was an old woman from Kent

____

____

____

____

Here lies the result of my labour

____

____

____

____

Understanding

Write an answer to each question.

a. Do you think a limerick is fun to write? Why? ______________________

____

b. What is the most challenging thing about writing a limerick? ______________________

____

c. What area of learning helped you to understand how to write limericks? ______________________

____

d. How can limericks be best enjoyed by the class? ______________________

e. What do you need to understand to write a limerick? ______________________

Interpreting

Circle **T** (True) of **F** (False) to answer each question.

a. Limericks are usually about people and are funny. **T** **F**

b. It is important to test the rhythm of words you use in a limerick. **T** **F**

c. Some lines don't rhyme in a limerick. **T** **F**

d. Limericks are named after a town in Ireland. **T** **F**

e. Limericks can be tested by clapping each line. **T** **F**

Grammar

Phrase OR Clause? **Remember:** A phrase doesn't have a verb but a clause does.

Write on the line whether each of the following is a phrase or a clause.

a. which came early ______________ **b.** before much longer ______________

c. down by the track ______________ **d.** before we knew it ______________

e. around the bend ______________ **f.** from the shop ______________

g. check out the rules ______________ **h.** in no time at all ______________

Spelling

More Difficult Words to Learn:

reliable **enjoyable** **comfortable**
manageable **agreeable**

Alphabetical Order: Write each word in AO.

____

____

Homophones: Weight and Wait

Choose the correct homophone to complete each sentence.

a. We had to __________ for him to help carry the heavy __________ for us.

b. He had the __________ of the World on his shoulders.

c. There is a long __________ to get into the stadium so we just had to __________.

Word Building

Prefix 'dis' giving a negative meaning. Use double 's' when a word begins with 's'. Add 'dis' to each word.

a. content __________
b. similar __________
c. charge __________
d. approve __________
e. appear __________
f. own __________
g. belief __________
h. respect __________
i. figure __________

Punctuation

Contractions Write each of these in the shortened form.

a. they are	________	b. she will	________	c. shall not	________
d. were not	________	e. did not	________	f. who is	________
g. over	________	h. even	________	i. there is	________

Decimal Fractions

1. 0.85 to the nearest tenth __________
2. 867.2 - 538.4 = __________
3. $\frac{4}{5}$ = 0.4 True or False? True ☐ False ☐
4. $\frac{87}{100}$ = ______ %
5. What is the place value of 7 in 3.87? __________
6. Is 6.7 closer to 6 or 7? __________
7. Write $\frac{3}{5}$ as a decimal fraction. __________
8. Write 35% as a decimal fraction. __________
9. Write $\frac{3}{4}$ as a percentage. __________
10. 20% of $800 = $ __________
11. Remove the non-significant zeros from each number. Re-write the decimal.

a. 0.320	b. 0.740	c. 3.720
________	________	________
d. 0.1070	e. 70.450	f. 02.020
________	________	________

Working with Decimals

1. Add the decimals. Remember to keep the decimal points aligned (under each other).

a. 83.72 + 17.64 = ___ . ___	b. 435.22 + 176.89 = ___ . ___	c. 382.77 + 453.68 = ___ . ___
d. 623.33 + 127.84 + 215.55 = ___ . ___	e. 335.16 + 273.84 + 129.86 = ___ . ___	f. 671.53 + 247.33 + 167.79 = ___ . ___

2. Add each sum of money. Remember to keep correct place value for cents and dollars.

a. $3287.65 + 462.36 + 1285.99 = $ ___ . ___	b. $2561.75 + 3820.72 + 3179.06 = $ ___ . ___
c. $6348.56 + 217.77 + 80.56 = $ ___ . ___	d. $3725.86 + 873.94 + 2685.79 = $ ___ . ___

Why I Like to Visit My Grandmother

I can't think of anything I enjoy more than going to see my grandmother. She is the most amazing person who always has lots of things to tell me. I like to hear what she has been doing as much as she likes to listen to me. She is so cool! We sit together and fill each other in before we decide what to do next. Sometimes this takes an hour or two and I think it's time well spent because I get to hear about the exciting things grandma has been doing.

After we have caught up on each other's exploits we then set about deciding what to do during this visit. Do you know there are so many things we think of that it is impossible to do all of them in the one day? Of course we laugh about that and choose what will be possible to do during the remainder of my visit. I like it when we can do cooking. Grandma is the most amazing cook! And she lets me try new things which I really like. My grandmother is unbelievable! Yes, she is one of a kind and I am really lucky because, in my opinion, there are not many grandmas who let young kids into the kitchen to make a mess. I don't want to be messy but somehow this just happens when I cook. But grandma understands.

So there are a few of my reasons why I do like to visit my grandmother. I guess by now you are envious and wish you had such an understanding grandma. Well, believe you me, there are not too many grandmas like mine but if you have one too then you are as lucky as me.

Understanding

Shade the bubble for the best answer.

a. Which word best describes visiting grandma's?
- ◯ boring
- ◯ exciting
- ◯ interesting
- ◯ dull

b. How long does it take to decide what to do at grandma's?
- ◯ all day
- ◯ all week
- ◯ a few hours
- ◯ a few minutes

c. What does grandma understand best?
- ◯ cooking is messy
- ◯ children are messy
- ◯ making a mess happens
- ◯ it is easy to clean up the kitchen

d. What word can you substitute for 'exploits'?
- ◯ interests
- ◯ decisions
- ◯ adventures
- ◯ expectations

Interpreting

Write an answer to each question.

a. What is the best thing that happens at grandma's? ______________________________

____

b. How long are the visits to grandma's? ______________________________

____

c. What is considered as "an hour or two well spent'? ______________________________

____

d. What reason is given for someone being 'envious'? ______________________________

e. Why is grandma 'unbelievable'? ______________________________

____

Grammar

Gender and Personal Pronouns

Re-write each sentence. Change the plural pronouns to singular pronouns. Watch the tense.

a. They were going to get them but they were too late.

He was ______________________________

b. We will be home for dinner but don't expect us too early.

____

c. They took us to see them before going away.

____

Spelling

More Difficult Words to Learn:

experience **observe** **manage** **describe** **behave**

Change each word to a participle. Drop the 'e' and add 'ing'.

____

____

Syllabification: Write the difficult words in syllables.

____

____

Missing Letters: Fill in the missing letters.

a. d ___ s c r ___ b ___ **b.** ___ x ___ ___ ___ ___ ___ ___ ___ ___

c. ___ a ___ a ___ e **d.** ___ ___ ___ c ___ ___ b ___

Word Building

Words beginning with silent **'g'**

Match each word to its meaning.

gnome, gnat, gnash, gnarled, gnaw

a. to grind (the teeth) ______________

b. wrinkled ______________

c. to bite ______________

d. a small bat ______________

e. little, old man ______________

Punctuation

Commas in Lists and Phrases.

Place the comma correctly in each sentence.

a. When the boys played cricket Sam scored twenty runs Steve fifty-five Usman eighty and then it rained.

b. On the desk Ri had a red blue green brown purple yellow orange and black pencil.

c. Before long the bus pulled up at our stop and Merv Paul Matt Pat Simon and the coach alighted.

d. One bright Sunday morning in December several boats were cruising along the river.

Averages

1. Find the average height, mass or length of each group of people, goods and fish.

a.

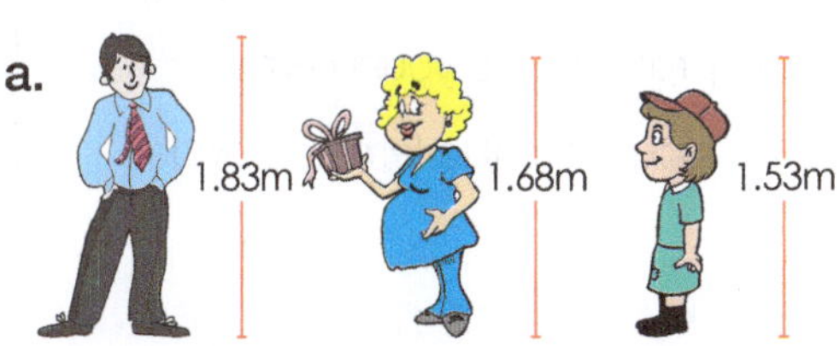

Family's average height ______ m

b.

4.3kg 3.2kg 4.5kg

Average mass ______ kg

c.

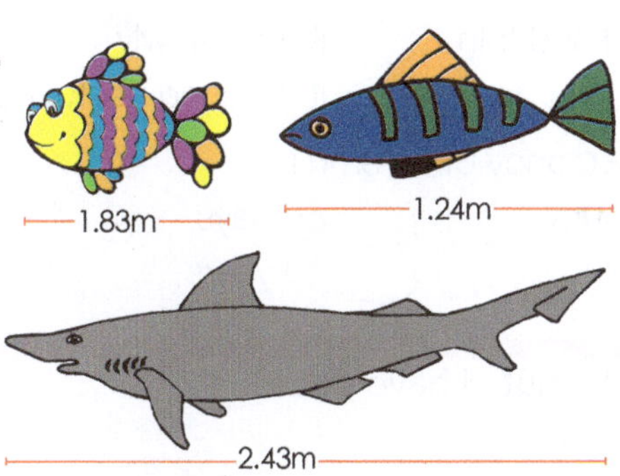

Average length ______ m

2. A car travels 240 kilometres in 3 hours.

What was its average speed per hour __________ km/h

Improper Fractions

1. Change the improper fractions to a mixed numeral.

a. $\frac{8}{5} =$ ___ **b.** $\frac{5}{2} =$ ___ **c.** $\frac{5}{3} =$ ___

d. $\frac{13}{8} =$ ___ **e.** $\frac{7}{4} =$ ___ **f.** $\frac{12}{5} =$ ___

2. Add the fractions. Write the mixed numeral.

a. $\frac{7}{8} + \frac{7}{8} = \frac{\square}{\square}$ ___ **b.** $\frac{4}{5} + \frac{4}{5} = \frac{\square}{\square}$ ___

c. $\frac{5}{8} + \frac{7}{8} = \frac{\square}{\square}$ ___ **d.** $\frac{5}{6} + \frac{3}{6} = \frac{\square}{\square}$ ___

3. Add each fraction. Find the lowest, common denominator first. Change improper fractions to mixed numerals.

a. $\frac{3}{4} + \frac{1}{2} =$ ___
$\frac{3}{4} + \frac{\square}{\square} = \frac{\square}{\square}$

b. $\frac{3}{4} + \frac{5}{8} =$ ___
$\frac{\square}{\square} + \frac{5}{8} = \frac{\square}{\square}$

c. $\frac{5}{8} + \frac{1}{2} =$ ___
$\frac{5}{8} + \frac{\square}{\square} = \frac{\square}{\square}$

d. $\frac{3}{4} + \frac{7}{8} =$ ___
$\frac{\square}{\square} + \frac{7}{8} = \frac{\square}{\square}$

Reading — The Emu — Unit 24

Information Report

The emu is the second largest bird in the World with the ostrich being the largest.

The female of the species is bigger than the male in both size and weight. It has wings but it can't fly and on the tip it has a small claw. It has a long neck and legs, which it uses to run at speeds up to 48kms/hour. Its feet have three toes and the sharp claws on its toes enable it to inflict wounds on opponents when fighting. Its bill is quite small but it has good eyesight and hearing allowing it to detect threats at some distance. The neck of the emu is pale blue and it has grey-brown , shaggy plumage. Both the male and female emu are of similar appearance.

The emu lives in a variety of habitats across Australia from the inland to the coast. It generally travels in pairs and often wanders great distances to feed. During the day it forages and preens its plumage. It can swim when necessary but usually does so if its habitat is flooded or it needs to cross a river.

It sleeps during the night for about 7-8 hours, only disturbing for short breaks. It makes various booming and grunting sounds mostly when it is mating season. The emu breeds during the summer months and the male makes the nest in a hollow on the ground from bark and grass, using sticks and leaves to line it before the female lays its eggs and the male incubates them. It takes about 56 days or eight weeks for the eggs to hatch and the male guards them for about seven months showing the chicks how to forage for food and to protect them from predators. An emu can live up to 10 years provided it is not attacked and killed by the Australian native dog – the dingo. Its other predator is the wedge-tailed eagle. Small chicks are often attacked by monitor lizards, red foxes, feral and domestic dogs and feral pigs. The emu eats insects, including grasshoppers and crickets, beetles, ants, spiders, cockroaches, ladybirds and a variety of native and introduced plant species.

The emu is a shield bearer on the Australian Coat of Arms with the red kangaroo. It also appears on the Australian 50c coin. In some areas of Australia it is at risk of extinction because of heavy logging and deliberate slaughter as well as from road-kill and the destruction of its eggs and the young by its predators.

Understanding

Tick the box if the information is in the text.

a. The emu is on the Australian Coat of Arms. ☐

b. The female Emu is larger than the male. ☐

c. Emus have three toes with sharps claws. ☐

d. The Emu sleeps for about 7 hours each night. ☐

e. Emus are attacked by the dingo. ☐

f. The male emu protects the young emu. ☐

g. Emus like to keep themselves looking good. ☐

h. The male emu incubates the female's eggs. ☐

Interpreting

Shade the bubble for the best answer.

a. To 'preen its plumage' means
- ◯ To look at its feathers
- ◯ To clean its feathers
- ◯ To dress its feathers
- ◯ To ruffle its feathers

b. How long does an emu take to incubate?
- ◯ 5 days
- ◯ 6 days
- ◯ 6 weeks
- ◯ 8 weeks

c. This information
- ◯ describes
- ◯ explains
- ◯ informs
- ◯ instructs

d. Which features best describe the emu?
- ◯ it is tall and thin
- ◯ it runs slowly
- ◯ its bill is large
- ◯ it has long neck and legs

e. A 'predator' is
- ◯ a friend
- ◯ a foe
- ◯ an enemy
- ◯ a killer

f. The life expectancy of an emu is
- ◯ 7-8 hours
- ◯ 56 days
- ◯ 8 weeks
- ◯ 10 years

Grammar

Helping Verbs in the Past Tense — I did but I have done

Cross out the incorrect verb forms in each sentence.

a. We (done/did) our homework last night.

b. He (rung/rang) the bell for lessons.

c. They (saw/seen) the emu at the zoo.

d. They (brang/brought) their iPad to school

e. He (had saw / had seen) it before.

f. She (has rang / has rung) the bell for school.

Spelling

More Difficult Words to Learn:
disagreement statement engagement incubation punishment

Change each noun to a verb.

____

____

Alphabetical Order: Write the challenging words in AO.

____

____

Dictionary Practice: Which word comes first?

a. knight or knave ________ b. knot or know ________ c. knead or knife ________

d. honour or honest ________ e. honorary or honorific ________ f. kneel or knelt ________

Word Building

Words beginning with silent letters – K and H

a. a dishonest fellow ________

b. truthful ________

c. a nobleman ________

Punctuation

Technical Terms and Single Inverted Commas

Write the meaning of each word.

a. 'habitat' ________ b. 'species' ________ c. 'incubates' ________

d. 'predator' ________ e. 'marsupial' ________ f. 'mammal' ________

Money

1. Write the discounted price for each item.

a. 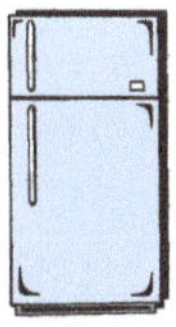 $890 less 10% off

Discount price ________

b.  $480 less 25% off

Discount price ________

c.  $36 less 25% off

Discount price ________

d.  $42 less 50% off

Discount price ________

2. Find the price of each item without GST. Remember to divide by 11 to get GST.

a.  $330 incl. GST

GST = $ ________

b.  $880 incl. GST

GST = $ ________

3 Jon wanted to buy a surf board. The tagged price showed $870 + GST. What was the price of the surf board with GST? $ ________

Multiplication

1. Find the product for each algorithm.

a. 793 x 4
b. 836 x 5
c. 728 x 3
d. 586 x 7
e. 368 x 6
f. 496 x 2

2. Use the extended form to find the product of each four-digit algorithm multiplied by a two-digit number.

a. 3724 x 23
b. 5815 x 34
c. 1362 x 25
d. 5164 x 38
e. 6125 x 27
f. 4153 x 46

Autumn Leaves by CT

A carpet of leaves lies blown to the ground
The wind howling strongly, creating the sound
Of branches bending boldly, touching the ground
Their leaves in a whirl, dancing merrily around.

Green and gold are their starting points
But soon they become
Red then purple and finally brown
In silent pursuit of their place on the ground.

They dance in the morning and flutter along
Gathering speed, showing many a hue
That belongs to nature and men can't do
In any attempt to pay them their due.

Make no mistake the season can do
What no earthly artist is able to do
But given your talent maybe you can
Reflect that colour on a scale so grand

Because autumn colours are certainly rich
Those fallen leaves, lying dead in the ditch
Provide us with colours spectacularly bright
Created by nature to enhance our delight.

Understanding

Shade the bubble for the best answer.

a. "The wind howling strongly" is an example of
- ◯ alliteration
- ◯ metaphor
- ◯ personification
- ◯ onomatopoeia

b. Which word gives the leaves human qualities?
- ◯ howling
- ◯ dancing
- ◯ flutter
- ◯ carpet

c. Which word is used to describe the leaves?
- ◯ noisy
- ◯ colour
- ◯ dead
- ◯ silent

d. Who is able to portray the colour of the leaves?
- ◯ an artist
- ◯ you
- ◯ nature
- ◯ autumn

Interpreting

Write an answer to each question.

a. Write the alliteration in this poem. ____________________

b. What is it that "men can't do"? ____________________

c. Who wrote this poem? ____________________

d. Why doesn't the second last verse have a full stop at the end of it?

____

e. What is the meaning of "showing many a hue"?

____

Grammar

Figurative Language – Personification and Metaphors

From the poem write two examples of personification.

a. ____________________ **b.** ____________________

Write one example of a metaphor. ____________________

Write on the line if the following is a metaphor or personification.

a. The wind howled then screamed with all its might. ____________________

b. The hunter had the heart of a lion. ____________________

c. He is a rough diamond. ____________________

Spelling

More Difficult Words to Learn:

explain **add** **violate** **relate** **moderate**

Nominalisation: Change each verb to a noun.

Use the suffixes – tion, ion or ation.

____

____

Antonyms: Add a prefix to form a word with an opposite meaning.

Write the word opposite in meaning to:

a. agree ____________ **b.** print ____________

c. correct ____________ **d.** perfect ____________

e. regular ____________ **f.** easy ____________

Word Building

The Prefix 'contra' meaning against.

Match each word to its meaning and write the word on the line.

contraband contrary contradict

contrast contract contravene

a. difference ____________

b. awkward ____________

c. to speak against ____________

d. violate ____________

e. an agreement ____________

f. unlawful, prohibited ____________

Punctuation

Abbreviations

Write the abbreviated form of:

a. Friday ____________ **b.** road ____________

c. you will ____________ **d.** shall not ____________ **e.** avenue ____________

Re-write this using correct punctuation.

f. i read the book thief in the holidays said valentina

____

Location

1. Give the co-ordinates for each shape on the grid.

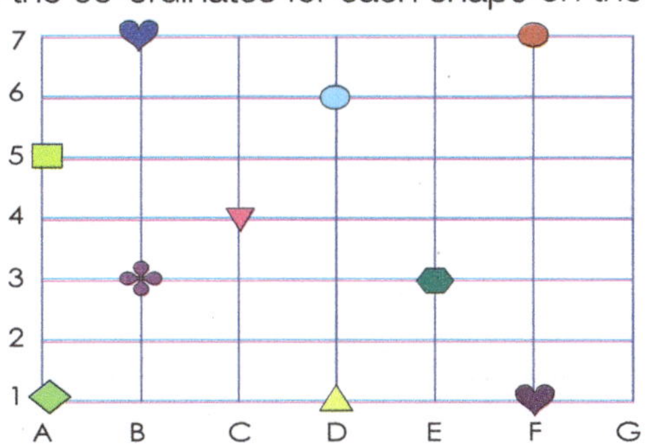

1. ____________ 4. ____________ 7. ____________

2. ____________ 5. ____________ 8. ____________

3. ____________ 6. ____________ 9. ____________

10. ____________

2. Complete the directional rose. Add the bearings too.
Use the bearing bank.

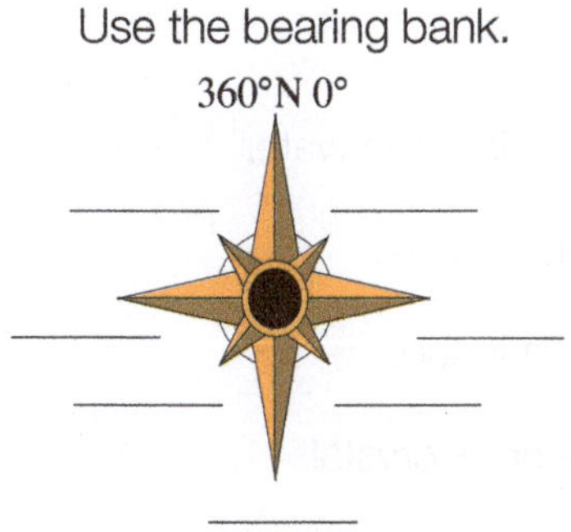

BEARINGS

45° NE

90° ____ 225° ____

135° ____ 270° ____

180° ____ 315° ____

Probability and Combinations

1. Use the word bank to help label the scale of probability.

0 ....

0.25 ....

0.5 ....

0.75 ....

1

Word Bank
possible
certain
impossible
unlikely
50-50

2. Answer the questions below and complete the diagram.

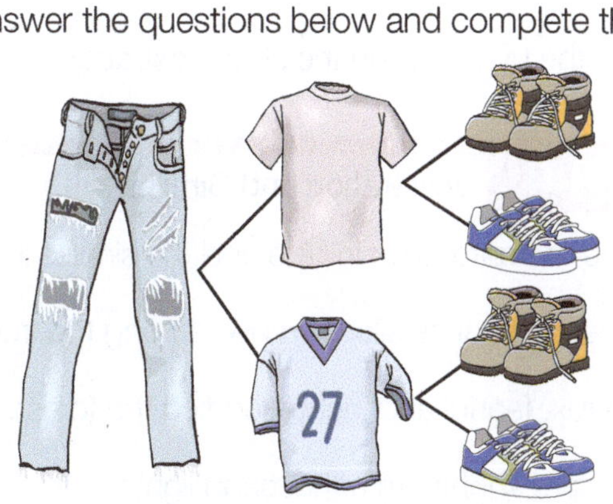

How many different combinations of clothing are possible?

A Terrific Tall Tale by U R Good

The waves were bigger than Mount Everest but that did not stop the man and his elephant trying to swim across the river. After all he knew he would make history if he achieved the impossible and reached the other side unscathed. Then again, there was no other way out now that he was committed to this particular crossing.

Can you believe it? That is the beginning of A Terrific Tall Tale and I promise you the rest of the book holds just as many hair-raising experiences. You can expect the man and his elephant to capture your imagination so much so that you will actually feel as though you are on the journey with them.

Find out how many of the most outlandish and untoward events are in this book and catch up with the characters when they land in more trouble than could be expected of one person and his companion to realise in a life-time.

When you get to the end of this book you will want to start all over again and go on some of the amazing and at times, terrifying and death-defying climbs and ground-breaking records of human and animal endurance. Believe me! I know what suspense is like and this book holds it all for you to experience.

A Terrific Tall Tale is about the close relationship between a man and his animal and how they make their way through many dangerous and unexpected terrains and rugged but vibrant landscapes.

Understanding

Circle **Yes** or **No** to answer the question.

a. This story is fiction. Yes No

b. You might find this in the library. Yes No

c. Would you read this book? Yes No

d. There are two people in the 'Tale'. Yes No

e. Does the book have suspense? Yes No

f. Would the author be well-known? Yes No

g. This plot is in a city. Yes No

h. The story is a fable. Yes No

Interpreting

Write an answer to each question.

a. Who might be interested in this type of book? ______________________

b. Where do you think this story happens? Explain your reason. ______________________

____

c. Why would you choose to read this book? ______________________

d. How has the review influenced your thinking about the book? ______________________

____

e. Write the hyperbole in the above extract. ______________________

Grammar

Alliteration and Similes

Underline the alliteration in blue and the similes in red in the sentences.

a. Slithering snakes silently move among the trees.

b. The cunning crocodile crept into the water.

c. The fox, fearful and frightened fled the forest.

d. A Terrific Tall Tale told terrible twists.

e. The stars shone like a thousand lights.

f. The Earth spun like a top let loose.

g. She is as calm as the ocean.

h. It was like the water, as clear as crystal.

Spelling

Unit 26

More Difficult Words to Learn:

active **reliable** **consolable** **enthusiastic** **necessary**

Change add 'in' or 'un' to each word to form its opposite.

____

____

Alphabetical Order: Write the difficult words in alphabetical order.

____

____

Missing Letters: Complete each list word.

a. __ e __ i a __ __ e **b.** __ n __ h __ s __ a __ t __ c

c. __ c __ i __ e **d.** __ __ c __ s __ __ __ __

e. __ o __ o __ __ b __ e

Word Building

Words with the long vowel sound of "I"

Read and say each word:

high, night, invite, digest, knight, kite

Now write some more:

____

____

____

____

____

____

Punctuation

Statement, Question or Command.

Mark the correct punctuation for each sentence.

a. did you see the new foal in the paddock

b. go for it cried the trainer

Write if each sentence is a statement, question or command.

c. There will be no play until the rain stops. ______________

d. "When will you be ready?" asked the leader. ______________

e. So get going, before it's too late! ______________

Pascal's Triangle

PASCAL'S TRIANGLE

1
1 1
1 2 1
1 3 3 1
1 4 6 4 1
1 5 10 10 5 1
1 6 15 20 15 6 1
1 7 21 35 35 21 7 1

TOTALS

a.	
b.	
c.	
d.	
e.	
f.	
g.	
h.	

1. Write the sum of each line of the triangle.
2. Write the triangular numbers showing on Pascal's Triangle.

3. Add the two triangular numbers that give each square number. (Look at Pascal's triangle).

a. ☐ + ☐ = 4 **b.** ☐ + ☐ = 36

c. ☐ + ☐ = 9 **d.** ☐ + ☐ = 25

e. ☐ + ☐ = 16 **f.** ☐ + ☐ = 49

Division

1. Complete each number sentence. Do the brackets first.

a. $(7 + 5) \div 4 =$ ☐ **b.** $(8 + 2) \div 5 =$ ☐

c. $(42 \div 6) + 7 =$ ☐ **d.** $(7 + 2) \div 3 =$ ☐

e. $(37 - 16) \div 7 =$ ☐ **f.** $(12 \div 2) + 2 =$ ☐

g. $(12 + 4) \div 2 =$ ☐ **h.** $(36 \times \frac{1}{2}) \div 6 =$ ☐

2. Complete each division algorithm. Write the remainder as a fraction.

a. 2)5135 r **b.** 4)6143 r **c.** 5)4362 r

d. 10)7137 r **e.** 4)5165 r **f.** 5)6273 r

3. Write the remainder to each division to two decimal places.

a. 4)5317.0 r **b.** 3)4528.0 r **c.** 5)3821.0 r

Come One – Come All – To Our School Fete

The pupils of **SMITHTON PUBLIC SCHOOL** invite you

____

to attend the **ANNUAL SCHOOL FETE**
to be held in the school grounds (weather permitting)

on: **FRIDAY, 22 NOVEMBER**

From: **5:00PM TO 9:00PM**

All activities will transfer to the School Hall in inclement weather.

Understanding and Interpreting

Design your own poster for the fete.

There are more important details that should be included on this poster: the type of stalls, activities to do, special competitions, lucky dips, rides, face painting etc. See how creative you can be and design a poster to cover all these aspects.

Grammar

Genders of Nouns – Feminine or Masculine

Write the **feminine** gender of these nouns:

a. hero __________ **b.** colt __________ **c.** wizard __________

d. buck __________ **e.** boar __________ **f.** fox __________

Write the **masculine** gender of these nouns.

g. peahen __________ **h.** aunt __________ **i.** cow __________

j. niece __________ **k.** bride __________ **l.** duck __________

Spelling

Word Families: **mortgage mortgagee mortgagor negotiate negotiator**

Syllabification: Write each word in syllables.

____

____

Word Meaning: Match each word to its meaning.

mortgage, mortgagee, mortgagor, negotiate, negotiator

a. Secure payment of a debt ________

b. The one owing a debt ________

c. One who lends on a secured debt ________

d. One who settles disputes ________

Word Building

Synonyms – Words with the Same Meaning.

Here are groups of words with an odd one out.
Write the odd one out on the line.

a. big, enormous, stretch, huge ________

b. wander, wonder, roam, ramble ________

c. lovely, beautiful, ugly, attractive ________

d. happy, sad, glad, joyful ________

e. mighty, strong, small, big ________

f. vibrant, colourful, vivid, dull ________

g. friend, foe, enemy, rival ________

h. king, queen, monarch, duke ________

Root Words: Greek "Chronos" meaning 'time'

Match each word to its meaning: **chronology, chronicle, chronic, synchronised**

a. continuing for a long time. ________

b. the order of past events ________

c. occurring at the same time ________

d. a record of events in time ________

Punctuation

Italics for Titles

The titles of books, songs, poems, plays or films, can be shown in italics or inverted commas.

Eg., Cinderella or 'Cinderella'

The title of the book in Unit 26 is *A Terrific Tall Tale*. or The title of the book in Unit 26 is '*A terrific Tall Tale*'.

Write the titles for Unit 14 and Unit 19 in this book using italics for each title.

a. ________ **b.** ________

Time and Timetables

1. Write the adjusted time for each situation.

a. A train is to arrive at 7:54 am.
It is 43 minutes late.
What time will it arrive? ________

b. The bus left the midnight run 11 minutes early.
Write its departure time
in 24-hour time. ________

2. Write each digital, 24-hour time as am or pm time.

a. 

b. 

c. 

________ ________ ________

3. Write the analogue times in 24-hour, afternoon time.

a. 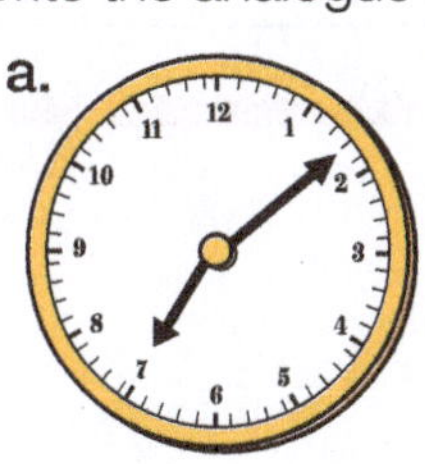

b. 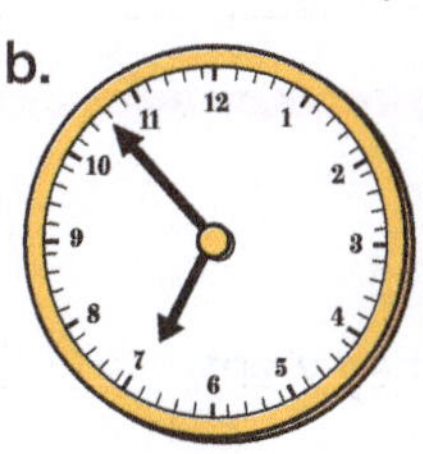

c. 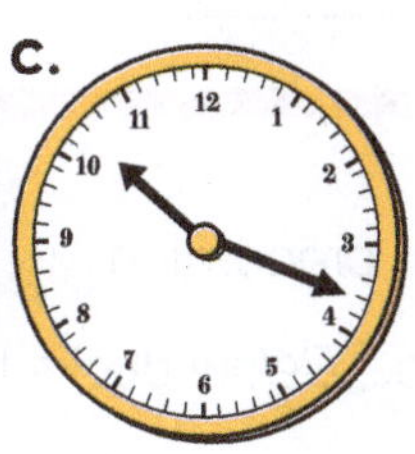

________ ________ ________

Fractions

1. Find the related common denominator for each fraction and then add the fractions.

a. $\frac{1}{2} + \frac{1}{3} =$ $\square + \square = \square$

b. $\frac{1}{5} + \frac{1}{2} =$ $\square + \square = \square$

2. Add these fractions. Change the improper fractions to a mixed numeral.

a. $\frac{1}{2} + \frac{3}{4} =$ ____ $\square + \frac{3}{4} = \square$

b. $\frac{4}{5} + \frac{2}{3} =$ ____ $\square + \square = \square$

3. Find the related common denominator for each fraction and then find the difference.

a. $\frac{4}{5} - \frac{1}{2} =$ $\square - \square = \square$

b. $\frac{3}{4} - \frac{1}{3} =$ $\square - \square = \square$

The Sun, the Earth and the Moon

The Sun is a million times bigger than the Earth. If you think of the size of the dome on the Queen Victoria Building in Sydney then, by comparison, the Earth would be just about as big as a football. The Sun is nearly 150 million kms from the Earth so it takes 8.5 minutes for the sunlight to travel from the Sun to the Earth.

The Sun speeds through space at 250km per second. That means it can travel the distance from Sydney to Orange or Melbourne to Hobart or from Launceston to Bendigo in one second. If you were to travel to the Sun in a jet aeroplane it would take you 19 years to get there.

The Sun is composed mainly of gas hydrogen. The Sun generates massive heat and the temperature at its core is 15 000 000°C and on its surface it is approximately 6 000°C. This is far hotter than anything we can generate on Earth. So it is easy to see why the Sun's power is being used to generate electricity for our homes today. In recent times it has become a popular way to power up our homes and it is a free source of energy.

The Earth orbits the Sun at nearly 30km per second. It takes one year for the Earth to orbit the Sun and one day to spin around on its axis. Beneath the crust of the Earth is molten lava and at the core the temperature is about the same as the surface of the sun – 6 000°C.

The Moon rotates on its axis once every 28 days (a Lunar month) and it orbits the Earth every 28 days too. This means the same side of the Moon is always facing the Earth. During the day the Sun warms the Moon up to 100°C– hot enough to boil water. At night the temperature plummets far below zero making it twice as cold as an Antarctic winter. There is no air on the Moon and astronauts who have travelled there had to wear special suits that kept them provided with oxygen.

On 20 July 1969 two American astronauts, Neil Armstrong and Edwin (Buzz) Aldrin landed on the Moon. If you were to fly to the Moon in a jet aeroplane it would take you 2 weeks 3 days and 8 hours to get there. But you would take about 4 days in a spacecraft.

Understanding

Shade the bubble for the best answer.

a. How long does it take the Moon to circle the Earth?
- ◯ 1 day
- ◯ 28 days
- ◯ 30 days
- ◯ 365 days

b. The Moon's daytime temperature is?
- ◯ 0°C
- ◯ 1°C
- ◯ 10°C
- ◯ 100°C

c. How long does it take the Earth to orbit the Sun?
- ◯ 1 day
- ◯ 28 days
- ◯ 30 days
- ◯ 365 days

d. The Earth's core temperature is?
- ◯ 100°C
- ◯ 1,000°C
- ◯ 6,000°C
- ◯ 15,000,000°C

e. Which of these is NOT found on the Moon?
- ◯ air
- ◯ minerals
- ◯ Nickel
- ◯ iron

f. Which statement is correct?
- ◯ The Sun orbits the Earth
- ◯ The Earth orbits the Moon
- ◯ Earth is smaller than the Sun
- ◯ The Sun is closer to Earth than the Moon

Interpreting

Write an answer to each question.

a. How far is the Sun from the Earth? ____________

b. How fast does the Sun travel? ____________

c. What is the Moon's day-time temperature? ____________

d. How hot is the Sun's surface? ____________

e. When did man first land on the Moon? ____________

f. The night temperature on the Moon is ____________

g. Why is the Sun a good source of power? ____________

h. How long does it take the Earth to orbit the Sun? ____________

Grammar

Adverbs and Prepositions

Write if the word in italics is used as a.) an adverb or b.) a preposition.

a. He jumped *off* the pier. ____________

b. *Below* decks they went. ____________

c. We went *out* last night. ____________

d. It was *out* of control. ____________

e. We lit a candle *in* the dark. ____________

f. Jump *in*! ____________

Spelling

More Words to Learn:

Industry **country** **necessity** **boundary** **literacy**

Change the 'y' to 'I' and add 'es' – to form Plurals

____

____

Syllabification: Write the list words in syllables.

____

____

Word Building

Greek Word **"hydro"** meaning Water

a. a vessel which lifts above the water is a ____________.

b. colourless, odourless, inflammable gas is ____________.

Proof Reading: Write each word correctly on the line.

a. kuntrie ____________ **b.** litracy ____________ **c.** bowndrie ____________

d. nigosheate ____________ **e.** moregage ____________

Punctuation

Quotation within a Quotation.

Here is an example: "Have you seen the new 'Star Wars' movie yet?" asked our uncle.

Write each sentence correctly.

a. did the latest pitch perfect dvd arrive yesterday asked jan

____

b. we sailed on the carnival spirit to new caledonia said valentina

____

Time and Timetables

1. Write the eight-digit number represented on each abacus.

a.

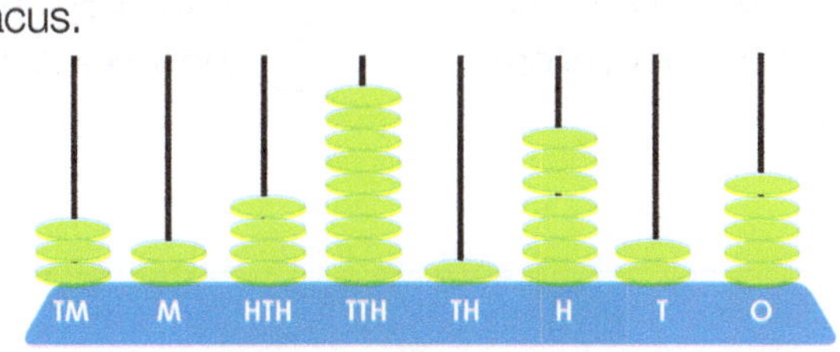

b.

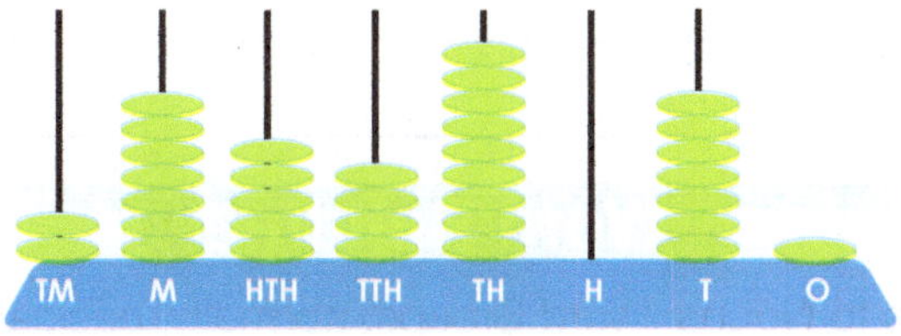

2. What is the place value of one in question 1.a.?

3. Arrange 2,8,7,6,1,4,3,0 to make the **largest** possible number.

4. Round off 93 817 600 to the **nearest** ten million.

Fractions

1. Change each mixed numeral into an improper fraction.

a. $3\frac{1}{2} = \square$ **b.** $1\frac{3}{4} = \square$ **c.** $2\frac{4}{5} = \square$

d. $4\frac{1}{4} = \square$ **e.** $3\frac{1}{3} = \square$ **f.** $1\frac{7}{10} = \square$

2. Find the related common denominator to help complete each subtraction.

a. $\frac{3}{4} - \frac{1}{3} =$ ____ $\square - \square = \square$

b. $\frac{2}{3} - \frac{1}{4} =$ ____ $\square - \square = \square$

3. Change each mixed numeral into an improper fraction and then subtract. Change improper fractions to mixed numerals in the answers.

a. $\frac{4}{5} - \frac{1}{2} =$ $\square - \square = \square$

b. $\frac{3}{4} - \frac{1}{3} =$ $\square + \square = \square$

4. Change each improper fraction into a mixed numeral.

a. $\frac{9}{6} =$ ____ **b.** $\frac{7}{4} =$ ____ **c.** $\frac{8}{5} =$ ____

Reading **A Gala Performance** Unit 29 *Narrative*

"Great!" cried Cere. "Yippee!" was my response.

Bet you don't know what made us so excited? Well, let me tell you a thing or two that started this mad, crazy carry-on at my place. We had been asked to join the performers on stage at the Opera House for the grand opening of the School Spectacular Show in which we were showcasing our latest dance routine. It had taken us months to prepare and at one stage it looked unlikely that it would be ready in time, but we forged ahead and now that reality was upon us we found our excitement hard to contain.

We had made the costumes and practiced our choreography leaving nothing undone. Everything had been a struggle over the last few weeks because there were a lot of other important things we had to do at school but we kept pushing ahead and finally we made it. We were so excited it was unbelievable! Initially we had not been chosen in the cast and even though everything had been planned so well the unthinkable happened. One of the star performers went down with the chicken pox. Now, not only was there a need to replace her, but, there was a strong possibility that some of the other cast would succumb to the disease. That meant replacing the principal dancer and possibly others. With only a day to go, everything started to fall into place and all was ready for opening night. Just as our teachers were revelling in their luck the worst thing that possibly could happen – did. Yes, you've guessed it!

Another one of the main performers called in sick and so Cere and I were picked to perform. Just as well we had kept up our practice and we were ready for our big chance to shine.

Understanding

Shade the bubble for the best answer.

a. Why were the girls so excited?
- ◯ they were ready
- ◯ it was their turn
- ◯ they were picked
- ◯ someone was sick

b. Where was the performance to take place?
- ◯ at the school
- ◯ at the Town Hall
- ◯ at the local hall
- ◯ at the Opera House

c. How long was the preparation for the concert?
- ◯ days
- ◯ weeks
- ◯ months
- ◯ a year

d. What was the cause of their dismay?
- ◯ no costumes
- ◯ no stage
- ◯ no star performer
- ◯ chicken pox

e. How many understudies were needed?
- ◯ one
- ◯ two
- ◯ three
- ◯ four

f. When did the girls get chosen to perform?
- ◯ on opening night
- ◯ in the beginning
- ◯ the day before
- ◯ the week before

Interpreting

Write an answer to each question.

a. Why were two new performers chosen? ______________________

b. Why were those two new performers chosen? ______________________

c. What lesson can be learnt from this story? ______________________

d. What was the name of the show the performers were in? ______________________

e. What was so special about the event? ______________________

Grammar

Adverbs and Present Participles Complete each sentence beginning with an adverb followed by a present participle.

a. Quickly running ______________________

____

b. Steadily carrying ______________________

____

c. Suddenly knowing ______________________

____

Word Building

Adverbs to Nouns Word Groups: **normally, basically, consequently, awkwardly, dramatically, quickly, beautifully**

Change each adverb to a noun

____

____

____

____

Revision Exercises Unit 30

Word Building: Double the last consonant to add 'ing' to each word.

a. begin ________ **b.** plan ________ **c.** wrap ________ **d.** omit ________

e. clap ________ **f.** regret ________ **h.** travel ________ **h.** sun ________

Proof Reading: Re-write each of the following words correctly.

a. nite ________ **b.** ocassion ________ **c.** accomodate ________

d. embaras ________ **e.** abandened ________ **f.** woolen ________

Nominalisation: Write each word as a noun.

a. normally ________ **b.** critically ________ **c.** compare(v) ________

d. favour (v) ________ **e.** judge(v) ________ **f.** question(v) ________

Homophones ***Desert Dessert Bite Bight***

Use each one correctly in these sentences.

a. The ________ Rat is a film set in World War II. **b.** Don't ________ your tongue eating that.

c. The Great Australian ________ can be rough. **d.** We usually finish dinner with ________.

Choose the Correct Word in Brackets – Cross the incorrect word.

a. (May / Can) I have a piece of (them/ that) cake? **b.** Please put the pencils (into / in) the box.

c. (Wasn't / Weren't) there any ripe bananas left? **d.** He (rung / rang) to ask us about our dog.

e. Did you (brung / bring) your bag for swimming? **f.** They (done / did) their homework at school.

Punctuation: Dates and Numbers

Write the following dates and numbers correctly.

a. Your birthday ________ **b.** Christmas Day ________

c. New Years Day ________ **d.** Australia Day ________

Fractions

1. Show each fraction as a decimal.

a.
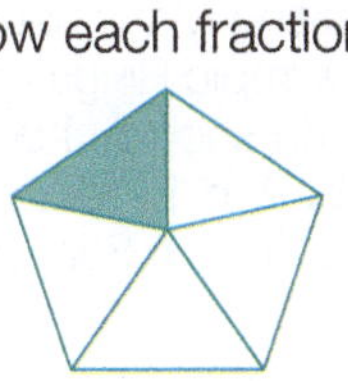
____

b.
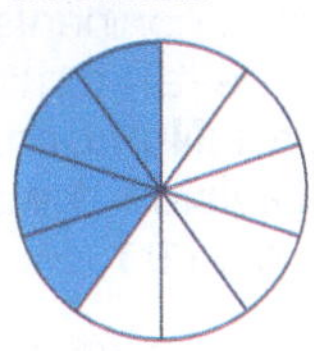
____

c.

____

2. Write each fraction as a decimal.

a. $\frac{1}{4}$ = ______ **b.** $\frac{2}{5}$ = ______ **c.** $\frac{7}{10}$ = ______

d. $\frac{3}{4}$ = ______ **e.** $\frac{1}{2}$ = ______ **f.** $\frac{6}{8}$ = ______

3. Write each decimal as a fraction.

a. 0.6 = ☐ **b.** 0.125 = ☐

c. 0.333 = ☐ **d.** 0.875 = ☐

Decimals

1. When subtracting decimals remember to keep the decimal points aligned.

a.	b.	c.
372.16	336.27	485.16
-157.29	-107.19	- 99.87
____ . ____	____ . ____	____ . ____

2. Paris' mother had \$160 to spend at the supermarket. Add the cost of goods and then calculate her change.

Vegemite	\$6.32
Cereal	\$5.97
Milk	\$3.95
Bread...................	\$4.64
Spent..................	\$

Change

\$160.00

Spend..... ________

Change \$ ________

Answers

Unit 1	**Understanding: a.** People are happy when they have a few of them. **b.** The senses used are touch, smell and sight. **c.** The notes are popular because of their colour, texture and smell. **d.** The note was put into a dark, smelly pocket and it finished up being washed. **e.** It is written in the first person. **Interpreting:** Circle - a. T b. T c. F d. T e. T **Grammar: a.** kangaroos; sheep; cattle; land; country; 1770; convict settlers; 1788; **b.** Australia; Captain Cook; British; Captain Arthur Phillip; First Fleet; **c.** mobs; flocks; **Word Building: a.** responsible **b.** serviceable **c.** comfortable; **d.** manageable **e.** convertible **f.** predictable **Spelling:** AO: attend, compare, generate, imagine, relax Nominalisation: attendance, comparable, generation, imagination, relaxation **Proof Reading: a.** circle bout; relax, verandah. We bought a new chair to relax in on the verandah. **b.** Circle good, description, thief. They have a good description of the thief. **Punctuation: a.** We came prepared, but they were ready for the party anyway. **b.** They said, "We will…**c.** You will need: three cups of sugar, … **d.** There were several books available, when the … **Rounding Off: 1 a.** 660 **b.** 840 **c.**380 **d.** 640 **e.** 720 **f.**550 **2a.** 700 **b.** 800 **c.** 400 **d.** 600 **e.** 700 **f.** 500 **3a.** 5 000 **b.** 6 000 **c.** 8 000 **d.** 6 000 **e.** 8 000 **f.** 5 000 **4a.** 16 000 **b.** 8 000 **Addition: 1 a.** 5 806 410 **b.** 407 568 **c.** 8 007 956 **2a.** 126 543 **b.** 171 683 **3a.** 90 916 **b.** 85 951 **c.**100 888
Unit 2	**Understanding:** Tick: a, b, c, d, f, g, h, i, j **Interpreting: a.** concealed **b.**deteriorated **c.** gradient **d.** fortifications **e.**sorely **f.**hordes **g.** eroded **h.**trenches **Grammar: a.** modern day **b.**invading **c.**stamped **d.** ancient **e.** two **f.** rammed **g.** steep **h.** First and Second Opium **i.** Mongol **j.** leg **k.**nine **Word Building: a.** sculptor **b.** surveyor **c.** teacher **d.** swimmer **e.** actor **f.** lawyer **Spelling:** Syllabification: con/fi/dence, gov/ern/ance, hes/i/tance, im/port/ance, re/li/ance Change: confide, govern, hesitate, import, rely **Punctuation:a.** It's .. **b.** I'll … **c.** They're.. it'll **d.** I'll **e.** mustn't **Place Value: 1 a.** 1 379 524 **b.**7 350 426 **2a.** 7 thousands **b.** 5 hundreds **c.** 4 hundred thousand **d.**8 ones **e.**3 million **3a.**6 254 004 **b.**7 443 817 **c.** 8 135 176 **Subtraction: 1a.** 3 215 **b.** 3 214 **c.**2 233 **2a.** 52 079 **b.**13 088 **c.** 55 779 **d.** 25 179 **3a.** $163.11 **b.** $330.85 **c.** $139.71 **4.** 4 877 sheep.
Unit 3	**Understanding:** Shade: **a.** 3 **b.** 2 **c.** 2 **d.** 3 **Interpreting: a.** The International Olympic Committee is in charge. **b.** Stadiums, swimming pools and athletic tracks as well as time, money and labour are all needed to host the Olympics. **c.**The first modern- day Olympics were held in Athens, Greece. **d.** At the closing ceremony doves are released. **Grammar: a.**celebration, imagination **b.**friendship **c.** wisdom, imagination, honesty **Word Building: a.**bee **b.**baby **c.**bird **d.**dog **e.**car **f.**person **g.**motor **h.** boy or girl **Spelling:** Change: judge, obey, punish, confide, attach **Dictionary Work: a.**maintain **b.**obedient **c.**question **d.** punished **e.** response **Punctuation: a.** icy-cold **b.**third-rate **c.** large-scale **d.** red-hot **e.**75-year-old **f.** second-class **g.** heavy-handed **h.** short-winded **Prime Numbers:** 3,5,7,11,13,17,19,23,29,31 **2a.** 1,2,4,8 **b.** 1,2,4,8,16 **c.** 1,2,3,4,6,8,12,24 **d.** 1,2,4,7,14,28 **3.** 8 **4.** 76 **Multiplication: 1 a.** 3 702 **b.**12 698 **c.** 19 025 **d.** 98 728 **e.** 198 762 **f.** 49 611 **2.** 978,/ 3 735, / 11 436,/ 2 571,/ 10 089,/ 12 843,/ 2 301
Unit 4	**Understanding:**Tick – a, b,c,d,e,f,g,h **Interpreting: a.** The International Olympic Committee organises the games. **b.**The colour of the rings represent one colour from each competing nations' flag. **c.**Yellow or green best represents Australia. **d.** This means the rings are a 'strong sign' of unity among the competitors. **e.**The cauldron is where the Olympic flame is burnt throughout the games. **Grammar: a.** like burning lava **b.** as thick as thieves **c.**as cold as ice **d.** like stone **e.** like boiling water **f.** like a snake **Similies:** Parent. **Word Building:a.** patriotism **b.** knowledge **c.** envious **d.** narcissism **Nouns: a.**quarry **b.**audience **c.** congregation **d.** catalogue **Spelling:** AO: attention, significance, sufficient, television, wondrous Change: signify, suffice, televise, wonder, attend **Proof Reading:** Circle: a. meny, athlets, competiting Many nations have athletes competing in the Olympic Games. **b.**deesined, reprsent, coninents. The Olympic Rings are designed to represent five continents. **Punctuation:a.** There could be rain tomorrow: you should check then. **b.**The Olympic Flag is white: it has five interlocking rings too. **Square Numbers: 1a.**4 **b.** 9 **c.**16 **d.**25 **e.**49 **f.**36 **2.**36, 100, 25, 64, 121, 81 **3a.**29 **b.**71 **c.**29 **d.**65 **e.**90 **f.**19 **Division: 1 a.**57 r1 **b.**151 r **c.**35r1 **d.**64r1 **e.**68r1 **f.**75r2 **2a.**169r2 **b.** 77r1 **c.**122 **d.** 214 **3a.**1 341 **b.**576r1 **c.**841r1
Unit 5	**Understanding:** Shade **a.**4 **b.** 2 **c.**4 **d.**1 **Interpreting: a.**Yes **b.**Parent **c.**Yes **d.** No **e.**No **f.**No **g.**Yes **h.**Yes **Grammar:** Match a/i, b/k, c/j, d/h, e/l, f/g. **Word Building:** NOTE:**a.** forward (no 'e'), **b.** forego **c.** forefinger **d.** forehead **e.** forecast **f.**foreshore **g.** foreclose **h.** foreshadow **i.** foresight **Spelling:** Nominalisation – attachment, conclusion, encouragement, favourable, acknowledgement AO: acknowledge, attach, conclude, encourage, favour **Missing Letters: a.** o,u,a,e,e **b.** a,o,e,e **c.** a,o,u,a,e **d.** o,u,e **e.** a,a **f.** e,o,u,a,e **g.** vowels **Punctuation: a.** S **b.** TD **c.** S **d.** O **Integers: 1a.** .7 **b.** 5 **c.** 7 **d.** 70 **2a.** +1 **b.**-4 **c.** -4 **d.** -5 **e.** -5 **f.** -3 **3a.**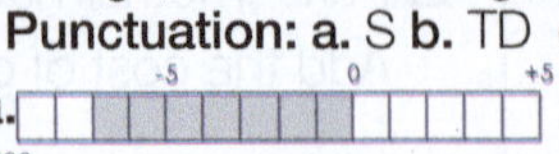 **b.** 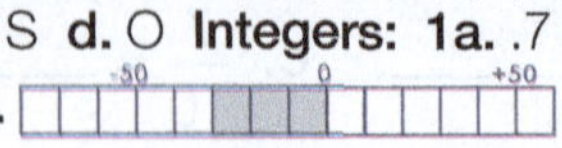 **c.** 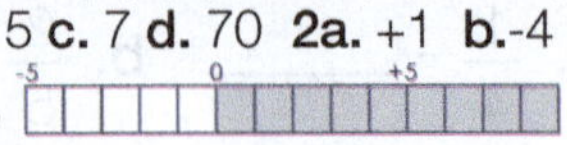 **d.** 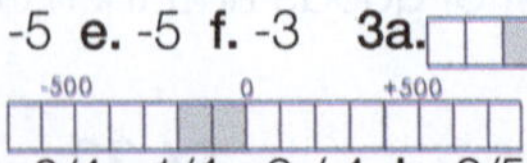 **Fractions: 1a.** 2/5 **b.**3/4 **c.** 3/5 **d.** 1/2 **e.**1/2 **f.** 1/4 **g.** 1/3 **h.** 1/4 **i.** 3/5 **2a.** 2/4 +1/4 =3 / 4 **b.** 2/5 + 1/10 = 5/10 = 1/2 **c.** 5/8 +2/8 = 7/8 **d.** 4/6 + 1/6 = 5/6 **e.**6/8 + 1/8 = 7/8 **f.** 3/10 + 4/10 = 7/10

Answers

Unit 6	**Understanding:** Shade:**a.**3 **b.**4 **c.**4 **d.**1 **Interpreting:** Circle: **a.**Yes **b.**Yes **c.**Yes **d.** No **e.**Yes **Grammar:** Parent **Word Building: a.** grandstand **b.** firewood **c.** goalkeeper **d.** broomstick **e.** understand **f.** fireworks **Spelling:** introduction, intention, imagination, information, limitation AO: imagine, inform, intend, introduce, limit **Scrambled Words: a.** introduce **b.** intention **c.** limit **d.** imagine **e.** intend **f.** inform **Punctuation: a.** (IOC) **b.** (RAM) **c.** (1916-2015) **Equivalent Fractions: 1a.** 1/10 **b.** 7/10 **c.** 5/10 or 1/2 **d.** 2/10 or 1/4 **e.** 6/10 or 3/5 **f.** 9/10 **g.** 3/10 **h.** 25/100 or 1/ 4 **i.** 75/100 or 3/4 **j.** 8/10 or 4/5 **2a.** 0.2 **b.** 0.4 **c.** 7/10 **d.** 20% **e.** 1/3 **f.** 0.4 **3a.** 0.5 **b.** 0.75 **Decimals and Fractions: 1a.** 0.3, 0.5, 0.6, 0.9 **b.** 3/8, 5/8, 3/4 or 6/8 **2a.** 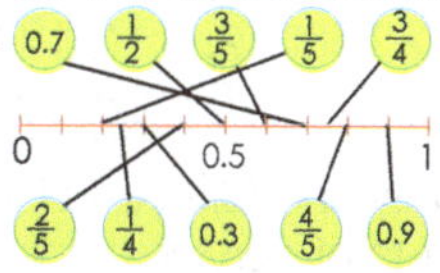 **3a.** 1/3 **b.** 2/5 **c.** 4/10 or 2/5
Unit 7	**Understanding:** Tick all **Interpreting: a.** The flag represents our ties to the British Empire, our laws, parliamentary democracy, freedom of speech and human rights and responsibilities. **b.** It represents our position in the southern hemisphere and relates to the Indigenous legends of Aboriginal and Torres Strait Islander peoples. **c.** The colour are red, white and blue. **d.** The cross of Scotland and Ireland are diagonal crosses. **Grammar:** Circle **a.** I, them **b.** he, she, them **c.** him, her **d.** you, they, you **e.** I **f.** it **Word Building: a.** submarine **b.** submariner **c.** subscribe **d.** subside **e.** subtitle **f.** subway **Proof Reading:** Circle & Write – **a.** capable, occasion **b.** fulfilled, bought, expensive **Spelling:** Antonyms: incapable, inattentive, unfulfilled, inexpensive, invisible **Dictionary Work: a.** available **b.** genius **c.** capable **d.** experience **e.** visible **f.** fulfilled **Punctuation: a.** Ben said, "Come here now!" **b.** "Why are you late?" asked dad. **c.** "Run quickly!" the boy yelled. **Money: 1a.**72% **b.**18% **c.** 48% **d.** 50% **e.** 75% **f.** 40% **g.** 70% **h.** 60% **i.** 25% **2a.** \$90 **b.** \$84 **c.** \$680 **d.** \$600 **Number Patterns: 1a.** 24 **b.** 36 **c.** 48 **d.**18 **e.**42 **f.**60 **2a.**122,174, 226 **b.** 81, 243, 729 **c.** 16,8,4
Unit 8	**Understanding:** Shade **a.** 2 **b.**4 **c.**2 **d.**4 **Interpreting:** Tick: a,b,c,e,f,h,i,j **Grammar: a.** a brute of a day **b.** this neck of the woods **c.** keeping a cool head **d.** anything that might be thrown at you **Word Building: a.** all-electric **b.** non-event **c.** all-important **d.** non-returnable **e.** non-smoking **f.** all-rounder **Spelling: Change**: wondrous, industrious, continuous, dangerous, famous AO: continue, danger, fame, industry, wonder **Missing Letters: a.** famous **b.** continuous **c.** dangerous **d.** industrious **e.** wondrous **Punctuation: a.** "Be careful not to slip," warned mum. " If you do…" **b.** "Watch out for trains!" cried the guard. "I don't want another accident." **Angles: 1a.** reflex **b.** right angle **c.** acute **d.** straight **e.** obtuse **f.** acute **2a.** 130° **b.** 55° **3a.** 55° **b.** 60° **c.** 40° **Mass: 1a.** 58kg **b.**3kg **c.**2kg **d.**150T **e.**1-1/2T **f.**500g **g.**20T **h.**2g **i.**5g
Unit 9	**Understanding:** Circle: **a.** Y **b.** Y **c.** Y **d.** Y **e.** Y **f.** Y **g.** Y **h.** N **i.** N **j.** N **Interpreting: a.** It means wet or rainy weather. **b.** There are two people with contact numbers to call. **c.** In the favourite character dress-up. **d.** For five hours **e.** The intended venue is the school grounds. **Grammar:** Suggestions: **a.** Depending on the weather, the school bazaar….. **b.** There will be lots of competitions involving different selections. **c.** Bring a chair or a rug so the family can enjoy a picnic. **Word Building: a.** duo **b.**dual **c.**duplex **d.** duet **Spelling:** Nominalisation: tolerance, abundance, significance, vigilance, observance AO: abundant, observant, significant, tolerant, vigilant **Dictionary Work: a.** abundant **b.** extravagant **c.** significant **d.** arrogant **Punctuation: a.** Commas after: weather, Friday **b.** clothes, cupboard **Length: 1a.**12m **b.**15cm **c.** 38mm **d.** 15cm **e.** 25mm **f.** 22m **2a.** 4cm, 46mm, 47mm, 42mm, 43m, 4km **b.** 9.89mm, 730cm, 7.87m, 0.7km, 0.72km, 780m **3a.** 52km **b.**44km **Distance and Time: 1a.**193km **b.** 363km **2a.** 100km **b.** 90km **3.**Parent.
Unit 10	**Understanding:** Shade **a.** 2 **b.** 3 **c.** 3 **d.** 4 **Interpreting:** Circle **a.** Y **b.** N **c.** Y **d.** Y **e.** N **Grammar:** Cross **a.** Whose **b.** who **c.** who **d.** who's **e.** which **f.** whose **g.**who's **h.** who **Word Building: a.** somewhere **b.** everywhere **c.** nowhere **d.** anywhere **Spelling:** Change: offering, developing, frightening, interrupting, entertaining AO: develop, entertain, frighten, interrupt, offer **Homophones:** s. cruise b.crews **Punctuation: a.** "The Man from Snowy River" is a well-known Australian poem. **Location: 1a.** A, 1-2 **b.** I-J 1-2 **c.** D-E 1 **d.** D-E 3 **e.** I-J 6-7 **f.** G 9-10 **2a.** Littleton Sports Oval, **b.** Littleton High School **3.** North/ West **Graphs: 1.** Parent **2.** Visual representation of each item **3.** Column graph, bar graph, line graph.
Unit 11	**Understanding:** Shade: **a.**4 **b.**3 **c.**3 **d.**4 **Interpreting:** Tick:a,b,c,d,e,g,h **Grammar: a.** kangaroo, powerful hind legs. **b.**buck, boomer, old man **c.**kangaroos, musky-rat **d.** kangaroo, Australian Coat of Arms **e.** Kangaroos, groups called 'mobs'. **Word Building: a.** burdensome **b.** wearisome **c.**quarrelsome **d.** troublesome **e.** worrisome **f.**wholesome **Spelling:** Rule: producing, measuring, increasing, gesturing, deciding **Missing Letters: a.**e,e,i,e,e, **b.**o,u,e **c.**e,a,u,e **d.**o,e,e **e.** i,e,a,e **f.** e,u,e **Homonyms:** a.b.c. suit **Punctuation: a.** Easter **b.**Christmas **c.**Ramadan **d.**Australia Day **e.**New Years Eve **Triangles: 1a**-equilateral, **b**-right angle, **c**-scalene, **c**-isosceles **2a.**12cm, scalene **b.**11cm, isosceles **c.** 9cm, equilateral **d.**12cm, right angle **Circles: 1a.** diameter **b.** sector **c.** arc **d.**semi-circle **e.**chord **f.**circumference **g.**radius **h.**sector **2a.** 5cm **b.**8cm **c.**7cm **3a.**semi-circle **b.** sector

Answers

Unit12	**Understanding:** Shade **a.** 2 **b.**1 **c.**4 **d.** 3 **Interpreting: a.** To learn skills, understand the water and to help them in the water. **b.**There are tree branches and submerged objects in rivers. å**c.** Swim between the flags when it is safe to do so. **d.**You should not swim alone or in a dangerous surf. **e.** Dams have slippery sides that can give way easily so it's hard to get out. **Grammar: b.** outside (where) **c.** there (when) **d.** between (where) **e.** quickly (how) **f.** after (when) **g.** because (why) **Word Building: a.** intercede **b.** intersect **c.**interject **d.** interview **e.** interfere **f.** intersperse **Spelling:** Syllabification: col/lo/qui/al, con/no/ta/tion, com/mun/i/ty, fa/cil/i/ties, im/me/di/ate **Dictionary Work: a.** colloquial **b.**connotation **c.** community **d.** facilities **e.** immediate **Homophones: a.**sweet **b.** suite **Punctuation:** parent. **Number Patterns: 1a.** 83.85, 8.385, 0.8385 **b.** 32, 128, 512 **c.** 565, 715, 865 **d.** 648, 612, 576 **e.** 200, 2 000, 20 000 **2.** 6,12,18,24,36,42,48,54,60,66,72, 78,84,90,96 **Fractions: 1.** Parent **2a.** 2/8 **b.** 6/8 **c.** 4/10 **3a.** 4/6 + 1/6 = 5/6 **b.** 5/8 + 2/8 = 7/8
Unit 13	**Understanding:** Shade **a.** 1 **b.** 3 **c.**1 **d.** 3 **Interpreting: a.** Grey and Glen Lea Streets **b.** south **c.**Marshall Street **d.**The museum **e.**About 750. There are not many streets or services in the village. **Grammar: a.** Yesterday, in the rain **b.**quickly, along the road **c.** inside, because of the cold **d.** quietly, before sunrise. **Word Building: a.** happy **b.** possible **c.** grammatical **d.** frequent **e.** absolute **f.** alternate **Spelling:** Syllabification: ben/e/fi/cial, al/ter/na/tive, pro/fes/sion/al, sit/u/a/tion, en/ter/tain/ment AO: alternative, beneficial, entertainment, professional, situation **Missing Letters: a.**b, n,f,c,l **b.**p.r.f.s,s,n,l **c.**l,t,r,n,t,v **d.**s,t,t,n **Punctuation:** a, c,e,f. **Place Value: 1a.** 19 million **b.** 72 million **c.** 89 million **d.** 44 million **2a.** ten thousands **b.** hundred thousands **c.**thousands **d.** hundred thousands **3a.**4 637 153 **b.**7 350 428 **Decimal Fractions: 1a.**0.7 **b.**0.5 **c.** 0.7 **d.**0.87 **e.**2 **f.** 1.385 **g.**1.083 **h.** 1.9 **2a.**0.2 **b.**0.7 **c.**0.4 **d.**0.75 **e.**0.625 **f.**1.5 **3a.**hundredths **b.**tenths **c.**thousandths
Unit 14	**Understanding:** Shade: **a.**3 **b.**2 **c.**1**d.**3 **Interpreting:** Tick all Grammar: **a.**Irma and Zac are playing cricket. **b.**Tomorrow it will rain so we will go to the cinema.**Word Building: a.** words **b.** ward **c.** tame **d.**earn crab **e.** a dead lie **Spelling:** Change: correspondence, dependence, adolescence, benevolence, malevolence. Syllabification: cor/res/pon/dent, de/pen/dent, ad/o/les/cent, ben/ev/o/lent, mal/ev/o/lent **Word Meaning: a.** malevolent **b.**dependent **c.**correspondent **d.** benevolent **Punctuation: a.** International Olympic Commttee **b.** International Cricket Committee **c.** National Rugby League **d.**Australian Football League **e.**Australian Rugby Union **f.**National Basketball League **Factors: 1a.**1,2,4,8,16 **b.**1,2,4,5,10,20 **c.**1,2,3,4,6,12 **d.**1,2,3,6,9,18 **2a.**T **b.**T **c.**T **d.** F **3a.**36 **b.**24 **c.**48 **d.**30 **Square Numbers: 1a.**16,9,25,36,81,64,9,100 **2a.**3^2-9, 9^2-81,7^2-49, 5^2-25, 2^2-4, 4^2-16, 6^2-36, 8^2-64, 10^2-100 **3a.**52 **b.**40 **c.**56 **4a.**72 **b.**33 **c.**32 **d.**48 **e.**28 **f.**16
Unit 15	**Understanding:** Circle: **a.**T **b.**T **c.**T **d.**F **Interpreting: a.** A large number of students walk to school and they have to cross the road. **b.** A member of the student council. **c.**The students would like to discuss the matter in more detail. **d.** It is important to have a foot crossing laid at the school's front entrance so students can cross the road safely and before there is another accident. **e.**It Is dangerous because there is no foot crossing in front of the school and students who walk to school need to be able to cross safely. **Grammar: a.** who is very busy **b.** which needs a safe crossing **c.**whose job it is to help us **d.** who broke his leg **e.** that we need **f.** to whom we spoke **Word Building: a.**of **b.**from **c.**off, of, from **Spelling:** Syllabification: ac/com/mo/date, ne/ces/sity, con/tin/u/ous, com/pe/ti/tive, e/vent/u/al **Proof Reading:** mayor, council, issue, their b. When, you, accommodate, your, resort **Punctuation: a.** Jump now! **b.** Don't' do that! **c.** Can you stop that! please **d.** I am not going! **e.** Not good Ali! **f.** Play the ball skipper! **g.** Will you go! **h.** It's not right! I tell you **i.** That's the house! The one on the hill. **Transformation: 1a.**  **b.** 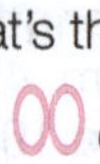 **c.**  **2a.** 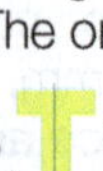 **b.**  **c.**  **d.**  **Chance: 1a.** ½ **b.** ½ **c.** 2/3 **2a.** 25% **b.**10% **c.**8% **3a.** red 40% **b.** blue 20% **c.** green 20% **d.** yellow 10%
Unit 16	**Understanding:** Circle **a.**Y **b.**N **c.**Y **d.**Y **e.**Y **Interpreting: a.** Bring Your Own Device **b.** First check to see if "insert" is active **c.** Windows **d.** A personal computer **e.** Parent **Grammar: a.** Those **b.** that **c.** that **d.** this **e.** these **f.** this **Word Building:** Parent check **Spelling:** AO: alcohol, chocolate, Christmas, lightning, vehicle **Dictionary Practice: a.** alcohol **b.** Christians **c.** lighten **d.** Islam **e.** vehicle **Punctuation: a.** Universal Serial Bus **b.** Random Access Memory **c.**Word Processor **d.** data base **e.** world wide web **f.** Read Only Memory **Area: 1a.** 12 cm^2 **b.** 8 cm^2 **c.**14 cm^2 **d.** 6cm^2 **2a.** 6cm^2 **b.** 4 cm^2 **Data: 1a.** Parent
Unit 17	**Understanding: a.** N **b.**Y **c.**Y **d.** Parent **e.**Y **Interpreting: a.** There will be lots of Barbie dolls for sale. **b.** Fruit and vegetables **c.** Not really. It is for a village. **d.** Parents and children. Most of the items are for them. **e.** Raj Sing **Grammar: a.** sang **b.** hurried **c.** howled **d.** grabbed **e.** slinks **f.** glided **Word Building:** Suggestions. **a.** truck **b.** buck/duck **c.** rack/sack **d.** backed/ lacked **e.** flicked **f.** tracked **g.** checked **Spelling:** AO: acquaint, brusque, colloquial, liquefy, ubiquitous. Note: Parent Missing Letters: **a.** b,u,i,o,u **b.** u,u,e, **c.** c,l,l,u,i,a **d.** a,u,n **Punctuation: a.** two-thirds **b.** twenty-seven **c.** one-half **d.** three and one-quarter **Volume and Capacity: 1a.** 250g **b.** 700g. **c.**1 000g (1kg) **d.**1 500g (1-1/2 kg) **e.** 550g **f.** 8 500g (8.5kg) **2a.** 3.75L **b.** 2.25L **c.**1.05L **d.** 0.35L **e.** 9.483L **f.** 0.795L **3a.**140g **b.** 400g **Number Patterns: 1a.**19,23,25 **b.** 36,49,64 **c.**15,21,28 **2a.** 29, 35,38,20,14,26,17,23 b. 21,12,19,7,11,15,9,13

Answers

Unit 18	**Understanding and Interpreting: a.** To assist in the planning and writing of the Term Three English tasks. **b.** An orientation, a plot, a complication and a resolution with a comment. Also, paragraphs with topic sentences and thinking, feeling and action verbs. **c.** The principal **d.** Research the details of migration to Australia after WWI. **e.** In the school library, on the Internet or the local historical museum. **f.** So people will want to read it. **g.** In the factual recount. **h.** The factual recount or the second assignment. **Grammar: a.** Yesterday First, then, Afterwards, before **Word Building: a.** swimsuit **b.** goal keeper **c.** commonwealth **Spelling:** Syllabification: a/bbrev/i/ate, in/ter/ro/gate, con/crete, cel/e/brate, mo/ti/vate Change: abbreviating, interrogating, concreting, celebrating, motivating **Dictionary Practice: a.** to question a person closely **b.** to move a person to action Correct: **a.** were, birthday, party **b.** bought, new, Wednesday **Punctuation: a.** wp **b.** db **c.** XL **d.** E-mail **e.** dvd **f.** mm **Factors:1a.** prime **b.**composite **c.**composite **d.** prime **e.** composite **f.** prime **g.** composite **h.** composite **2a.** 4,12,34 **b.** 9,12,27 **c.**10,25,75 **3a.** 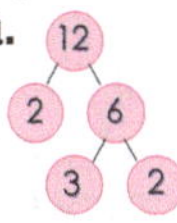 **b.** 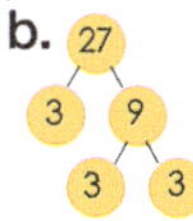 **c.** 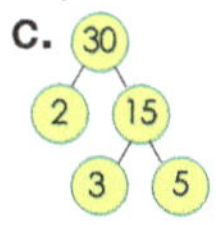 **Fractions: 1a.** 2/3 **b.** 2/3 **c.**1/3 **d.**4/5 **e.**3/5 **f.** 1/2 **2a.** 2-1/5 **b.**1-2/8 **c.**2-1/2 **d.**1-2/7 **e.**1-1/4 **f.**2 2/5 **g.**2 1/3 **h.**1 1/5 **3a.** 20% **b.**75% **c.**30% **d.**50% **e.**80%
Unit 19	**Understanding:** Shade **a.**4 **b.**4 **c.**2 **d.**1 **Interpreting:** Circle **a.**No **b.**Yes **c.**Yes **d.**Yes **e.**Yes **f.**Yes **Grammar: a.** waited, turned to bowl, missed **b.** were singing and dancing to enjoy **c.** go there to get **d.** was trying to lift **e.** tried to help carry **Word Building: a.** anti-clockwise **b.**ante–room **c.** anti-septic **d.** anti-meridian **e.** anti-venom **f.** anti-social **Spelling:** Antonyms: inedible, unavailable, unresponsive, unquestionable, invaluable **Homophones: a.** prey **b.** pray **c.**prayed **d.** preyed **Plurals: a.** mice **b.**teeth **c.** women **d.** feet **e.** children **f.** geese **Punctuation:** Parent **Place Value: 1a.** 62 539 445 **2.** 987 644 321 **3.** 48 million **4.** 39 million **5.** 38 247 964 **6.** 18 516 210, 23 417 602, 38 217 430, 49 324 788 **Addition: 1a.** 92 030 **b.**48 656 **c.** 60 444 **d.** 95 399 **2a.** $ 7 087.01 **b.** $13 705.50 **3.**159 206
Unit 20	**Understanding:** Shade: **a.**1 **b.**2 **c.**3 **d.**4 **Interpreting: a.** representative **b.** Parent **c.**Year 6 looks forward to having a dinner to say good-bye to each other and to celebrate their seven years of schooling. **d.** They are very important to ensure no one is left out. **e.** Because they make up the most number in the class. **Grammar: a.** mine, yours **b.** our, ours **c.** yours, his **d.** mine, his **e.** his, his **Word Building: a.** all-important **b.** all-electric **c.** non-event **d.** non-smoking **e.** ex-convict **f.** ex-serviceman **g.** half-hourly **h.** half-back **i.** self-made **Spelling:** Nominalisation: demonstration, hesitation, concentration, situation, education **Word Meaning: a.** hesitate **b.** demonstrate **c.** educate **d.** situate **Dictionary Practice:a.** demonstrate **b.** hesitation **c.** countersign **d.** slick **Punctuation: a.** an,an,the **b.** a,the,a **c.** a,a,the **Integers: 1a.**  (-3) **b.** (+2) **2a.** -5,-4,-3,-2,0,2,3,4 **b.**-4,-3,-2,0,1,2,3,6 **3a.** -4 **b.** +4 **c.**-2 Two-Digit **Multiplication:1a.** 16 821 **b.**11 375 **c.** 20 296 **2a.** 2 368 pieces **b.** 2 496 seats
Unit 21	**Understanding:** Circle **a.** Y **b.** Y **c.** Y **d.** Y **e.** Y **f.** Y **g.** Y **h.** N **i.** Y **j.** N **Interpreting: a.** www.mrbigmenswear.com.au **b.** Under the sizing guide menu. **c.** Double click on the word CLEARANCE in the left hand menu. **d.**Hamilton, NSW **e.**Pay with a credit card or Pay Pal. **Grammar:** Underline: **a.** have rung, will be **b.** has seen **c.**have been **d.** had been, could be **e.** has come **f.** have done **Word Building: a.** Parent check **Spelling:** Change: extravagance, arrogance, significance, tolerance, brilliance **Proof Reading: a.** mystery **b.** buried **c.** properly **d.** occasion **e.**ninety-nine **f.** scissors **g.** beautiful **h.** explosions **i.** tsunami **Missing Letters: a.** s,g,n,f,c,n,t **b.** t,l,r,n,t, **c.** b,r,l,l,n,t, **d.**r,r,g,n,t **Punctuation: a.**When I went to see Omar and Mustafa at Bankstown I caught the bus to Roselands first. **b.** You and I could go with Mark and Ari to see the new Star Wars show on Saturday. **Division:1a.**103r 2/5 **b.** 206r1/4 **c.** 212r1/3 **d.**120r1/7 **e.** 367r1/2 **f.**119r1/6 **2a.** $30 per hour **b.** 30kms/day **3a.** 588.25 **b.**1 074.4 **c.** 1 875.5 **d.** 305.2 **Time:1a.**16:05 **b.** 20:27 **c.**14:42 **2a.**11:45pm **b.** 7:30am **c.** 9:36pm **d.**3:50pm **3a.** 8 hours 35 mins **b.**4 hours 52 mins **c.**28hours 55mins
Unit 22	**Limericks** Parent Check **Understanding: a.** Parent **b.** Possible answer: Selecting a topic and keeping the rhythm in the lines. **c.** Music **d.** By saying them aloud together, or reading them aloud to the class. **e.**Rhyme and rhythm **Interpreting:** Circle: **a.**T **b.**T **c.**F **d.**T **e.**T **Grammar: a.** clause **b.** phrase **c.** phrase **d.** clause **e.** phrase **f.** phrase **g.** clause **h.** phrase **Word Building:** Parent check **Spelling:** AO: agreeable, comfortable, enjoyable, manageable, reliable **Homophones: a.** wait, weight **b.**weight **c.** wait, wait **Punctuation: a.**they're **b.**she'll **c.**shan't **d.**weren't **e.**didn't **f.** who's **g.**o'er **h.**e'en **i.** there's **Decimal Fractions: 1.** 0.9 **2.** 328.8 **3.**False **4.** 87% **5.**Hundredths **6.** 7 **7.** 0.6 **8.** 0.35 **9.** 75% **10.** $160 **11a.**0.32 **b.**0.74 **c.**3.72 **d.**0.107 **e.**70.45 **f.**2.02 **Working With Decimals: 1a.**101.36 **b.** 612.11 **c.**836.45 **d.**966.72 **e.**738.86 **f.**1 086.65 **2a.**$ 5 036 **b.**$9 561.53 **c.**$6 646.89 **d.** $7 285.59
Unit 23	**Understanding:** Shade: **a.**2 **b.**3 **c.**3 **d.**1 **Interpreting: a.** Various. Talking to Grandma. Being able to cook. Making a mess! **b.** A day **c.** Sitting talking to Grandma to hear about the exciting things she has been doing. **d.** Having an such an understanding Grandma. **e.** Grandma lets you choose what you would like to do and she doesn't mind if you make a mess. **Grammar: a.** He was going to get him but he was too late. **b.** I will be home for dinner but don't expect me too early. **c.** She took me to see her before going away. **Word Building: a.** gnash **b.** gnarled **c.** gnaw **d.** gnat **e.** gnome **Spelling:** Change: experiencing, observing, managing, describing, behaving **Syllabification:** ex|per|i|ence, ob|serve, man|age, de|scribe, be|have **Missing Letters: a.** e,i,e **b.** e,p,e,r,i,e,n,c,e **c.** m,n,g **d.**d,e,s,r,i,b **Punctuation:** Commas after – **a.** cricket, runs, five **b.**desk, red, blue, green, brown, purple, yellow **c.** long, Merv, Paul, Matt, Pat **d.** December **Averages: 1a.**1.68m **b.**4kg **c.**1.83m **2a.**80km/hr **Improper Fractions: 1a.** 1-3/5 **b.** 2-1/2 **c.**1-2/3 **d.**1-5/8 **e.**1-3/4 **f.**2-2/5 **2a.** 14/8=1 ¾ **b.**8/5=1-3/5 **c.**12/8=1-1/2 **d.**8/6=1-1/3 **3a.**5/4=1-1/4 **b.**11/8=1-3/8 **c.**9/8=1-1/8 **d.**13/8=1-5/8

Answers

Unit 24	**Understanding:** Tick a,b,c,d,e,f,g,h **Interpreting:** Shade: **a.**3 **b.**4 **c.**2 **d.**4 **e.**3 **f.**4 **Grammar:** Cross **a.**done **b.**rung **c.**seen **d.**brang **e.**had saw **f.**has rang **Word Building: a.** knave **b.** honest **c.** knight **Spelling:** Change – disagree, state, engage, incubate, punish AO: disagreement, engagement, incubation, punishment, statement **Dictionary Practice: a.**knave **b.**knot **c.**knead **d.**honest **e.** honorary **f.** kneel **Punctuation: a.** a living space **b.** type, or kind **c.**to sit on, to hatch **d.** one who robs or kills **e.**carries its young in a pouch **f.** suckles its young in a pouch **Money:1a.** $801 **b.** $360 **c.** $27 **d.** $21 **2a.**$30 **b.**$80 **3.** $957 **Multiplication:1a.**3 172 **b.** 4 180 **c.**2 184 **d.**4 102 **e.**2 208 **f.**992 **2a.** 85652 **b.**197710 **c.**34050 **d.**196232 **e.**165375 **f.**191038
Unit 25	**Understanding:** Shade: **a.**3 **b.**1 **c.**3 **d.**3 **Interpreting: a.**branches bending boldly **b.**Create the colours of the Autumn leaves. **c.**The writer of this book. **d.**It is meant to continue reading on to the next verse. **e.**Showing most of the colours of the spectrum. **Grammar: a.** the wind howling strongly **b.** they dance in the morning **c.**fallen leaves, lying dead in the ditch **a.** personification **b.**metaphor **c.**metaphor **Word Building: a.** contrast **b.**contrary **c.**contradict **d.**contravene **e.**contract **f.**contraband **Spelling:** Nominalisation: explanation, addition, violation, relation, moderation **Antonyms: a.** disagree **b.**misprint **c.**incorrect **d.**imperfect **e.**irregular **f.**uneasy **Punctuation: a.** Fri. **b.**rd **c.**you'll **d.**shan't **e.** ave. **f.**"I read The Book Thief in the holidays," said Valentina. **Location: 1.**B3 **2.**D6 **3.**E3 **4.**B7 **5.**C4 **6.**D1 **7.**F7 **8.**A5 **9.**F1 **10.** A1 **2.**90° East 135° SE, 180° South, 225° SW, 270° West, 315° NW **Probability and Combinations: 1.** 0-impossible, 0.25-unlikely, 0.5-50-50, 0.75 – possible, 1- certain **2.** 4
Unit 26	**Understanding: a.**yes **b.**no **c.**parent **d.**no **e.**yes **f.**no **g.**no **h.**no **Interpreting: a.** A person who likes adventure and suspense stories. **b.**In mountains and rivers and outback or arid areas. Because it has unexpected terrains and rugged landscapes. **c.**parent **d.**parent. Ideas: has suspense; is an adventure; Has an elephant as a character; And so on… **e.**The waves were bigger than Mount Everest. **Grammar:a.** slithering snakes silently **b.**cunning crocodile crept **c.**fox, fearful and frightened, fled **d.**terrific tall tale **e.**stars shone **f.** like a top let loose **g.**as calm as the ocean **h.**as clear as crystal **Word Building:** parent. **Spelling:** inactive; unreliable; inconsolable; unenthusiastic; unnecessary AO: active, consolable, enthusiastic, necessary, reliable **Missing Letters: a.** reliable **b.**enthusiastic **c.**active **d.** necessary **e.**consolable **Punctuation: a.** Did you see the new foal in the paddock? **b.**"Go for it!", cried the trainer. **a.**statement **b.**question **c.**command **Pascal's Triangle: 1**.1,2,4,8,16,32,64,128 **2.** 1,3,6,10,15,21 **3a.**1+3=4 **b.**21+15=36 **c.**3+6=9 **d.**10+15=25 **e.**6+10=16 **f.**21+28=49 **Division: 1a.** 3 **b.**2 **c.**14 **d.**3 **e.**3 **f.**8 **g.**8 **h.**3 **2a.** 2 567-1/2 **b.**1 535-3/4 **c.**872-2/5 **d.**713 7/10 **e.**1291 1/4 **f.**1254 3/5 **3a.**1 329.25 **b.**1 509.33 **c.**764.2
Unit 27	**Understanding and Interpreting:** Parent **Grammar:a.** heroine **b.**filly **c.**witch **d.**doe **e.**pig **f.**vixen **g.** peacock **h.**uncle **i.**bull **j.**nephew **k.**groom **l.**drake **Word Building:a.** stretch **b.**wonder **c.**ugly **d.**sad **e.**small **f.**dull **g.**friend **h.**queen **Syllabification:**mort|gage; mort|gag|ee; mort|gag|or; ne|go|ti|ate; ne|go|ti|at|or **Word Meaning: a.**mortgage **b.**mortgagee **c.**mortgagor **d.**negotiator **Root Words: a.** chronic **b.**chronology **c.** synchronised **d.**chronicle **Punctuation:a.***Volcanoes and Earthquakes* **b.***Rip Van Winkle* –**Time and Tables: 1a.**8:37am **b.**23:49 **2a.**1:27pm **b.**3:55pm **c.**6:02pm **3a.**19:08 **b.**18:53 **c.**22:18 **Fractions: 1a.**5/6 **b.**7/10 **2a.**5/4=1-1/4 **b.** 22/15=1-7/15 **3.**3/10 **b.**5/12
Unit 28	**Understanding:** Shade **a.**2 **b.**4 **c.**4 **d.**3 **e.**1 **f.**3 **Interpreting:a.**150m kms **b.**250kms/sec. **c.**1000C **d.** 6 0000C **e.**20-07-1969 **f.** zero **g.**Because it is so hot and it's free. **h.**1 year. **Grammar:a.** adverb **b.** adverb **c.**adverb **d.**preposition **e.**preposition **f.**adverb **g.**preposition **h.**preposition **Word Building: a.** hydrofoil **b.**hydrogen **Spelling:** industries; countries; necessities; boundaries; literacies; **Syllabification:** in|dus|try; coun|try; ne|cess|it|y; boun|dar|y; lit|er|ac|y; **Proof Reading: a.** country **b.**literacy **c.** boundary **d.** negotiate **e.**mortgage **Punctuation: a.** "Did the latest Pitch Perfect dvd arrive yesterday?" asked Jan. **b.**"We sailed on the Carnival Spirit to New Caledonia," said Valentina. **Place Value: 1a.**32 491 725 **b.**27 549 071 **2.**Thousand **3.** 87 643 210 **4.** 90 million **Fractions: 1a.** 7/2 **b.**7/4 **c.**14/5 **d.**17/4 **e.**10/3 **f.**17/10 **2a.**5/12 **b.**5/12 **3a.**8/10 – 5/10=3/10 **b.**9/12-4/12=5/12 **4a.**1-1/2 **b.**1-3/4 **c.**1-3/5
Unit 29	**Understanding:** Shade **a.**3 **b.**4 **c.**3 **d.**3 **e.**2 **f.**3 **Interpreting:a.** The star performer got sick. **b.** Because they had kept up their practice and knew the routines. **c.**Never give up. **d.** School Spectacular **e.**It was the grand opening at the Opera House. **Grammar:a. b. c.** parent **Word Building:** normal, basic, consequence, awkward, drama, quick, beauty
Unit 30	**Word Building: a.**beginning **b.**planning **c.**wrapping **d.**omitting **e.**clapping **f.**regretting **g.**travelling **h.** sunning **Proof Reading:a.** night **b.**occasion **c.**accommodate **d.**embarrass **e.**abandoned **f.** woollen **Nominalisation: a.**normal **b.**critical **c.**comparable **d.**favourite **e.**judgement **f.**questionable **Homophones:a.** Desert **b.**bite **c.**Bight **d.**dessert **Correct Word:a.** May that **b.**into **c.**Weren't **d.**rang **e.**bring **f.**did **Punctuation:a.** parent **b.**25 December **c.**1 January **d.**26 January **Fractions:1a.**0.2 **b.**0.4 **c.**0.5 **2a.**0.25 **b.**0.4 **c.**0.7 **d.**0.75 **e.**0.5 **f.**0.75 **3a.**6/10 or 3/5 **b.**1/8 **c.**1/3 **d.**7/8 **Decimals: 1a.**214.87 **b.**229.08 **c.**385.29 **2.** $20.88 change = $139.12